SEEDS OF JUSTICE

SEEDS OF JUSTICE

Organizing Your Church to Transform the World

ALEX TINDAL WIESENDANGER

ORBIS BOOKS

Maryknoll, New York 10545

ORBIS BOOKS
Maryknoll, New York 10545

Fathers and Brothers
MARYKNOLL.
TOGETHER IN GOD'S MISSION OF MERCY

Founded in 1970, Orbis Books endeavors to publish works that enlighten the mind, nourish the spirit, and challenge the conscience. The publishing arm of the Maryknoll Fathers and Brothers, Orbis seeks to explore the global dimensions of the Christian faith and mission, to invite dialogue with diverse cultures and religious traditions, and to serve the cause of reconciliation and peace. The books published reflect the views of their authors and do not represent the official position of the Maryknoll Society. To learn more about Maryknoll and Orbis Books, please visit our website at www.orbisbooks.com.

Library of Congress Cataloging-in-Publication Data

Names: Wiesendanger, Alex Tindal, author.
Title: Seeds of justice : organizing your church to transform the world / Alex Tindal Wiesendanger.
Description: Maryknoll, NY : Orbis, 2020. | Includes index. | Summary: "Practical tools for organizing communities and congregations to promote social change"—Provided by publisher.
Identifiers: LCCN 2019035902 (print) | LCCN 2019035903 (ebook) | ISBN 9781626983656 (paperback) | ISBN 9781608338290 (ebook)
Subjects: LCSH: Project management. | Church management. | Social change—Religious aspects—Christianity. | Christianity and justice. | Christians—Political activity.
Classification: LCC BV652.14 .W45 2020 (print) | LCC BV652.14 (ebook) | DDC 261.8—dc23
LC record available at https://lccn.loc.gov/2019035902
LC ebook record available at https://lccn.loc.gov/2019035903

Contents

Appendixes

Introduction

Why does the world we hear preached about on Sundays seem so different from the one we see in our lives Monday through Saturday?

What do we do with the anger we feel watching the news, scrolling through social media feeds, or just walking down the street because of the unfairness and injustice we see?

How do I to get my congregation involved in the issues I care about?

Can my church actually create real change in laws and policies that deeply violate the gospel?

Is there more than intercessory prayer and peace marches that my parish can be doing?

If these are questions you ask yourself, then maybe this book is for you.

I began organizing because I wanted real answers to these questions, and this book is the record of what I've found through more than fifteen years of work, many mistakes, and the guidance of a number of more experienced mentors and everyday church and community members and leaders.

I grew up during the 1980s and '90s on the border of Spanish Harlem and Harlem, rough neighborhoods at the time. It was an odd place to grow up as a white family, witnessing the struggles of our black and brown friends and neighbors, while also, because of our racial and cultural privilege, remaining largely exempt from many of the burdens they carried. Seeing this disparity got me started in the world of social justice, marching and protesting, even before I had a full analysis of what was going on or any real training or methodology on how to effect change.

Trying to answer these questions led me to participate in the AFL-CIO's Union Summer program in Kansas City, organizing with construction workers for their rights during the day and canvassing neighborhoods around economic justice issues in the evenings. From there, I joined the Jesuit Volunteer Corps and moved to Tennessee to combat the death penalty. Inspired by this fight, I ended up staying long past my volunteer year. Speaking at churches, organizing legislative campaigns, and planning rallies and vigils was right up my alley. Despite being a real youngster in the fight, I was entrusted with vital work and we were able to pass the first anti–death penalty legislation in Tennessee's modern history. I saw the abolition movement as the point of the spear in taking on racism and mass incarceration.

But I also became painfully aware that fighting around a single issue, even one as morally compelling as capital punishment, had its limits. Not enough people felt the issue in their guts on a day-to-day basis, meaning that we would always be in the position of moral suasion, hoping that those in power would hear the righteousness of our arguments. Otherwise, we didn't really have the ability to make change happen when they didn't. We had plenty of passionate, radical activists on our side, but we weren't touching a large swath of the general public.

I wanted to build something strong enough to actually compel action and change. And I wanted to learn how to become more deeply ingrained in the life of congregations and communities.

This led me to the Community Renewal Society (CRS) in Chicago, a storied social justice organization, with deep roots in the civil rights movement. There, for over eight years, I worked first as an organizer and then as the director of organizing, under the guidance of the Rev. Calvin S. Morris, PhD, an icon who had served on the staff of Dr. Martin Luther King Jr. Over the years at CRS, we developed tools to engage not just individuals but entire churches. I went from leading demonstrations of a few hundred people to working with congregational leaders to create public actions of thousands. In my years there, our organizing helped create change in the city, the county, and the state, often around issues that no one was talking about and where elected officials had been unable to move in the past.

We passed legislation to create job opportunities for people with felony records. We helped fight for a fair state budget with more equitable school funding for low income students. We built a coalition that unlocked $20 million for affordable housing. We combatted violence and mass incarceration, creating community-based restorative justice peace hubs. And during this time, we learned how vital whole congregations, not just individuals, are, and how, by doing the work of justice, we can transform congregations themselves.

Several years ago, I left CRS. Now married with two young children, my wife and I had decided to begin a process (which took longer than we thought it would) to move back to our home city of New York. In the intervening years, I've had the privilege to continue to organize exciting efforts for justice in a number of roles: as the national organizing director for Jobs to Move America, a community and labor coalition focused on leveraging our public infrastructure spending to create economic, racial, and environmental justice; as the campaign director for the Responsible Budget Coalition in Illinois, a coalition of more than three hundred organizations that finally succeeded in ending the longest budget impasse in U.S. history and in leading the charge for a progressive income tax amendment to the Illinois constitution; and now as the international lead organizer for the American Federation of Musicians, fighting to ensure that multinational corporations like Disney and Live Nation don't make profits on the backs of working musicians. And at the urging of many friends and collaborators, I also took time to begin working on this book, knowing that the tools we had learned were needed by so many congregations and communities.

This book is broken into three large sections corresponding with the major movements that we and our congregations need to undergo to become real agents of change. These are (1) understanding our call, (2) preparing our churches, and (3) taking action for change. Each section includes a number of chapters, each focusing on a different specific lesson and set of skills. And, because no real change is ever accomplished alone, each chapter also includes, in their own words, a story from a lay leader, community member, or clergy person about how they have used these tools to create real change in their congregations and communities—just as you can in your own.

In the first section of this book, we need to understand our call. We are called to act, not just for charity and mercy for the oppressed, but for justice. Jesus calls us to be radicals, in the true sense of the word, meaning to go to the roots. We are called to change the very structures of our society. And to do so, we must get comfortable with power, both individually and as congregations. These movements aren't easy for most of us to make. We might not think of ourselves as radicals, and we may shy away from power. Our congregations may not feel ready for this either, but, with the foundation of our faith and solidarity together, we can move forward.

The second, and longest, section of this book is focused on this movement itself. How do we and our congregations actually become powerful and prepare ourselves to create change. Jesus spent most of his time preaching in the countryside and preparing his disciples before his final march to Jerusalem and his confrontation with the Roman Empire and its collaborators among Jewish leadership. Musicians and athletes spend many hours practicing and preparing before public performance. But faith-based justice efforts so often simply identify an issue and attempt to spring into action without any of the work necessary to be successful. This was the insight I have gained from the labor movement, and it's the specific tools of congregational organizing that will allow our churches to move into action and do so powerfully, faithfully, effectively, and in unity.

Finally, we turn to our public witness and action itself and address how churches can act to create real change in our communities. As people of faith we must accept that following Jesus will bring us into conflict with those in power. We need to let go of many of the fears and false teachings that hold us back. And we need to learn how to create plans and strategies to use our newfound power to succeed.

The miraculous thing about God's work is that, so often, while we are calling out to God to create a miracle, waiting for a prophet to arrive, God is quietly letting us know that we already have what we need. The seeds of our congregational transformation are already there, planted in our hearts' desire to see our world made new. What we must do is water and cultivate these seeds, growing ourselves and our churches into what we want them to be, what God desires for our world, communities of love, justice, and transformation. We, in fact, are the people we have been waiting for. All that is left to do is to begin.

PART I

Understanding Our Call

CHAPTER 1

God Has Anointed Us
to Bring Good News to the Poor

Do you remember the first time that you noticed injustice, that there was something wrong or unfair going on?

For me, it was starting first grade. I had been accepted into a special "gifted and talented" program at a public school a bit downtown from our apartment on the border of Spanish Harlem and Harlem in New York City. My father was a mailman, and my mother was trying to make a career as a stage manager in the theater, so we didn't have a lot of money, making Harlem one of the few areas (at that time) that we could afford to live and still be in Manhattan. We definitely stuck out a little, this white family living right at the intersection of these Latino and black neighborhoods. But as a young kid I didn't notice a lot of that or ascribe any special significance to it, until it was time to go to school.

One of the first things I noticed in my class was how overwhelmingly different my classmates looked from my friends in my neighborhood. Despite the fact that this was a public school, the kids who had been labeled "gifted and talented" were overwhelmingly white, with some Asian children, and almost no black and brown students. And our school looked different from the schools in my neighborhood as well. The Anderson program at P.S. 9, was great. We had roomy classrooms with clean desks, and eighteen or twenty kids in each class. We had a gym, a nice yard for recess, and a science lab. The school was colorful and clean.

The schools in my neighborhood, and even the nonselective middle school across the street, looked very different. There were metal gratings across the windows and metal detectors on the doors. I knew my friends had as many as thirty kids in a class and frequently didn't even have enough books for each student to get to take one home.

As I started making friends and getting invited on play dates, I noticed how different the apartments of my classmates were from ours, and certainly from the apartments where my friends from the neighborhood lived in. My classmates lived in big spacious apartments (by New York City standards) full of nice things—shiny, new refrigerators and dishwashers, fancy game systems. And their streets didn't look anything like the gritty streets that I was used to. I even noticed that some parents were happy to have me over to play but didn't want their kids coming over to our house. I remember my best friend's mother several years later insisting that he take a cab door to door if he was coming to our house, even though there was a bus that ran on an almost identical route.

Over the years, I could see these differences add up. I was learning things in class that my friends weren't. I was going on field trips and having music lessons that they didn't have available to them. At six or seven years old, I didn't know words like structural racism and social injustice. But I could tell that something wasn't fair here. My classmates weren't necessarily smarter than my neighborhood friends, but there was very different treatment happening.

What was going on here?

Noticing something unfair in the world happens to most of us at some point. Maybe you saw different schools, like I did. Or maybe it was noticing homeless people on the street. Maybe traveling between neighborhoods or between the city and the suburbs for the first time, looking out a car or bus window, you saw how different the houses looked. But whatever it was, at some point most of us notice that things are unequal.

And for some of us, God uses this noticing to nudge us into action.

We aren't alone in feeling this tug. In fact, it is at the heart of the Christian message. In the Gospel of Luke, Jesus is baptized, hears the voice of God declare him to be God's beloved son, and then is tempted in the desert for forty days and forty nights. When he returns, he heads to a synagogue and stands up to launch his public ministry that will change the world; he begins by quoting these words from scripture:

> The spirit of the Lord is upon me, because God has anointed me to bring good news to the poor. He has sent me to proclaim freedom for the prisoners and recovery of sight for the blind, to set the oppressed free, to proclaim the year of the Lord's favor. (Luke 4:18-19).

This is Jesus's first public statement, his mission statement, if you will, his announcement of what he is here to do. I've always felt called to this scripture, and given this location I think these lines are particularly worth looking at if we are going to follow Jesus. So what does he say?

Well, first of all, there is that phrase "proclaim the year of the Lord's favor." What is that about? To my twenty-first-century ears, that always sounded like simply a nice sounding phrase. But in first-century Israel, it had a specific meaning. The year of the Lord's favor meant the jubilee.

Again, to us, centuries and thousands of miles away, jubilee has come to just mean a big party, and why not? Jesus is here! Let's boogie down! But that is not what the jubilee actually meant to the hearers of Christ's time. It was a prescription of actions that the Jewish people were meant to follow once every fifty years which included all debts being forgiven, all slaves and prisoners being freed, and all land being returned to its original owner. It was a radical redistribution of wealth, from those who had much, back to those who had little, ensuring that the riches of the land could not accrue more and more, generation by generation, to a select few. So when Jesus proclaims the year of the Lord's favor in a first-century synagogue in occupied Israel, everyone in the temple would have understood that he was calling for a very concrete and radical set of reforms.

And he doesn't stop there. He wants to free prisoners and end oppression. He is here to provide healing to those who are sick and disabled. And he is here with good news for the poor. Now I suppose you could argue that the good news has nothing to do with our world here on earth, that the tidings of great joy are that nothing is going to get better in this life, but that, if you accept your fate, there is a better world for you in the next one. But this seems unlikely to me. First of all, it would hardly be in keeping with the rest of the passage, which clearly deals with very concrete, earthly changes. And second, if the good news is about the next life, why would Jesus proclaim this exclusively to the poor? Heaven and salvation are good news for everyone.

In fact, what always strikes me about this passage is that Jesus does not refer to creeds of belief or personal salvation at all! That is not to say that Jesus's life and work were not concerned with these things, but we do have to note that Jesus's kickoff to his ministry is talking about real, tangible earthly change.

In doing so, Jesus is locating himself squarely within the tradition of the Hebrew prophets, who called on the Jewish people, and especially the leaders, to act with justice toward the poor and helpless. Throughout the Bible and Jesus's subsequent ministry, God calls on God's people to care for the least of these, the *anawim*. In fact, it is Jesus's most frequent topic, and over two thousand lines of scripture refer to caring for the poor. But what form should that care take? The prophet Micah, in another of our best-known passages, very clearly answers the question of what God demands of us:

> He has told you, O man, what is good;
> And what does the Lord require of you
> But to do justice, to love mercy,
> And to walk humbly with your God? (Micah 6:8)

This famous scripture, and hundreds more like it, offers the two feet for walking the Christian path in the world—the foot of justice, or righteousness, and the foot of mercy, or charity.

We could spend whole chapters or whole books (and people have) describing and defining these terms, but over the years, I have come to a few basic criteria:

Charity deals with the effects of injustice	Justice deals with root causes of injustice
Charity focuses on the needs of individuals	Justice focuses on changing systems
Charity does not challenge the status quo	Justice challenges the status quo and exposes conflict.

Let's take those one at a time.

Root Causes or Effects

Have you ever heard the parable of the babies in the river?

Imagine if you live in a small town by a river. Upstream from you there is a bend in the river, and imposing cliffs, so no one from your town has ever been very far up river. Just past your town, the river gets choppy and leads to a waterfall. Now imagine one day you are by the river and you see a baby floating down the river. Obviously if it keeps going it will go over the waterfall, so you do what anyone would do, you jump in the water and pull the baby out and bring it to shore. Since you have no idea where the baby may be from, you bring it into your own house to care for it. But a little bit later, you see something else in the water and realize that it's another baby! Again you jump into the water and bravely pull it out. Maybe you take this baby to your neighbor to see if they can take care of it. But by now, you and your townsfolk are getting worried. You station someone by the river night and day, and realize that babies are coming down all the time. There is more need than you ever realized! As a good Christian town, you spring into action. You create a citizens' lifesaving brigade to be by the river all the time. You build a hospital for tend to babies' medical needs, a school and nursery to take care of them, and an adoption program to begin placing the babies with loving families in your village. You feel deeply called to this work and justifiably proud of all the amazing things that your town is doing.

But there is a big question left unasked: what is going on up river? Someone needs to go upstream, navigate the rapids and cliffs, and find out why babies keep ending up in the river in the first place!

This seems obvious, but think how often our churches see a need and respond to it for years and years without asking these questions. How many years have you been participating in the annual habitat for humanity trip or hunger walk? At the same time, has your church been going up river to ask why so many people are without food or adequate housing in the first place? The work of justice calls us to go upstream and ask this foundational question.

And asking this question also points us to the second distinction between charity and justice.

Individual Needs or Systems Change

As I shared at the beginning of the chapter, at a young age I realized that my friends and I were being offered very different educational opportunities, and, very quickly, this could be seen in our educational attainment. More and more of the children in my neighborhood were falling behind in school. A lot of good faith-based people might respond to this with tutoring programs for children from under-resourced schools, backpack giveaways, and bake sales to raise funds for new books or equipment. And these are all great initiatives. But they also focus our work on meeting the immediate needs of the children for educational support. The work of justice looks at how we change a system that doesn't allocate resources fairly.

For example, in America, we have made a choice to primarily fund schools through local property taxes. What this means is that wealthier areas, because of their higher levels of wealth and property values, are able to allocate far more money to public education than low income areas. And because housing loans were denied to people of color for generations, the homeownership gap between people of color and white people also means that basing school funding on local property taxes will continue to contribute to and exacerbate racial inequality. When I moved to Chicago and began to work with churches about the issues they were most concerned with, the issue of unequal education came up almost immediately. A wonderful pastor I worked with had grown up in Maywood, a low-income, primarily African-American suburb just west of the city. She remembered how she had seen so many children denied the basic resources to succeed, while just a few miles away, other children went to school on luxurious campuses. "Alex, we have to do something about school funding," she insisted to me.

What we discovered was that, in Illinois alone, a child that went to school from kindergarten through high school in one of the state's lowest income districts, where kids already often faced a number of really serious barriers and challenges, would have over $150,000 less spent on their education than a child who went from kindergarten to twelfth grade in one of the state's wealthiest districts—$150,000 difference on each child's education. We had made a choice to create a system that perpetuated and deepened unequal opportunity.

The work of justice is about understanding the systems that create injustice and focusing our work on transforming those systems to create just outcomes. In the book of Isaiah, the prophet addresses the rulers of the Hebrew people: "Woe to you who make unjust laws and the writers who keep writing oppression, to turn aside the needy from justice and rob the poor of my people of their rights" (Isaiah 10:1-2). The work of justice challenges the powers and principalities of our society to make laws and policy that align with God's call to put concern for the least of these first.

Status Quo or Challenge

This distinction tends to be the one that upsets people the most. This is not to say that charitable work cannot be transformative in addressing the needs of people, even large numbers of people, or cannot truly turn someone's life around. It can. But the work of charity or mercy accepts the status quo in terms of injustice and then tends to the needs that it produces. Pope Francis's image of the church as a "field hospital for the wounded" is a beautiful image. The people working at a field hospital do vital, dangerous, and heroic work to save lives. But they don't spend their energy challenging the reason for the war itself. Justice, on the other hand, must challenge and question the status quo, or as the famous liberation theologian, Archbishop Dom Helder Camara of Brazil said, "When I give food to the poor, they call me a saint. When I ask why the poor have no food, they call me a communist."

As Archbishop Camara's statement demonstrates, doing the work of justice exposes conflict. I use the word "exposes" here very intentionally, because when people begin to raise issues of justice, they will almost always be accused of creating conflict. But the fact is, that conflict already exists. Injustice and oppression are forms of conflict. The work of doing justice simply means asking the questions that bring that conflict and injustice to the surface. In 1963, Dr. Martin Luther King wrote his famous "Letter from a Birmingham Jail," partly in response to the critique of white clergy that he was creating conflict. But, as Dr. King explained, "I am in Birmingham because injustice is here." He goes on to explain that they must create the constructive tension and not wait:

Perhaps it is easy for those who have never felt the stinging darts of segregation to say, "Wait." But when you have seen vicious mobs lynch your mothers and fathers at will and drown your sisters and brothers at whim; when you have seen hate filled policemen curse, kick and even kill your black brothers and sisters; when you see the vast majority of your twenty million Negro brothers smothering in an airtight cage of poverty in the midst of an affluent society . . . when you take a cross-county drive and find it necessary to sleep night after night in the uncomfortable corners of your automobile because no motel will accept you; when you are humiliated day in and day out by nagging signs reading "white" and "colored"; when your first name becomes "nigger," your middle name becomes "boy" (however old you are) and your last name becomes "John," and your wife and mother are never given the respected title "Mrs."; when you are harried by day and haunted by night by the fact that you are a Negro, living constantly at tiptoe stance, never quite knowing what to expect next, and are plagued with inner fears and outer resentments; when you are forever fighting a degenerating sense of "nobodiness"—then you will understand why we find it difficult to wait.

In other words, we are all already in conflict and the victims of conflict. Doing the work of justice simply means making it impossible for those in power and those who are comfortable with injustice to ignore that conflict any longer. Injustice creates conflict; justice exposes it and challenges the status quo to resolve the conflict by ending the injustice. A leader I've worked with a great deal, Jiquanda Nelson, shares her story:

Why I Founded the Zion Minority Caucus

If I had to summarize what community organizing means to me, I'd say one (hyphenated) word: Life-changing. Because organizing has done just that—it's changed my entire life.

Having grown up in a two-parent home in a culture and community that was seeing more single-parent homes and higher poverty, giving was just what we did. We were constantly feeding hungry children, giving rides to those whose family couldn't afford a car or caring for our friends whose parents worked many jobs or countless hours to survive. So, when my fifth-grade teacher offered our class the chance to volunteer at the local PADS (Public Action to Delivery Shelter) program working with people experiencing homelessness, it was no surprise that I signed up every week.

My experience helping at the PADS shelter launched me into a life of charity. Throughout high school, I volunteered for many organizations. In college, I started a mentoring program for a local middle school and tutored high school athletes. While it was great work, it was at times disheartening because I was spending only four hours a week with the children, but they went back to broken homes, violent communities, and lives filled with hopelessness. The more I volunteered, the more I felt this weird void. And I didn't know why.

Right after college, my pastor invited me to a congregational organizer training where the facilitator walked through the difference between charity and justice. Charity impacts the individual and justice impacts the system. At that moment, this ideology gripped me. That was the void! Up until then, I was only doing work that impacted the individual when my drive felt more connected to impact the entire system. I spent too much work trying to feed the hungry when there was a burning desire within me wanting to know, "Why, in one of the wealthiest nations, are there so many who are hungry?"

Using this new understanding, I first became an active leader with my church and the Community Renewal Society and then worked to found the Zion Minority Caucus. During our first few months of doing the work, we already had some important wins. We won resources for a recreation center that serves children and families in the lower economic area of our community but often an afterthought by park district leadership. We also received commitments from our local chief of police following a police-involved shooting death of a black man for important reforms in our police department's culture, training, and accountability protocols.

Although I've shifted my focus, I'm not doing more work than I was doing before. It was simply a matter of choosing. Did I want to do charity and continue putting a Band-Aid on issues that were impacting my community? Or would I spend my time in the social justice space, doing the work that changes the lives of my children and their children's children. For me, the choice was clear. I'm spending my energy focusing on work to change systems!

Charity and justice are two sides of the same coin, and we can approach issues from both directions. Many churches are really concerned with the issue of homelessness. It hits a lot of us right in the face as we walk to work or get on the train or bus. Think about how we might go about tackling this issue.

How could your church engage the issue of homelessness from a charitable perspective?

Many churches engage in work like food pantries and soup kitchens that directly feed people experiencing homelessness. Others participate in shelters or programs that open the church up to allow people experiencing homelessness to sleep in the church. When I was living in Nashville, I got to see an amazing program called Room at the Inn that housed hundreds of people experiencing homelessness at dozens of different area churches every night; it was a truly inspiring ministry. Other churches participate in angel trees or clothing drives. I'm sure you can think of even more ideas.

Going a little deeper, some churches engage in more holistic charitable ministries. They work with Habitat for Humanity or a similar organization to actually build new housing for families in need. Or they create job training ministries to help prepare people for new careers. They may sponsor AA groups to support people in recovery. These kind of programs still address the needs of individuals but do so in a deeper or more permanent way, akin to the old saying "Give a man a fish and he eats for a day, teach him how to fish and he eats forever."

All of these responses are important and can mean literally life and death for people living at the margins of our society. But, in the end, they still focus on the needs of individuals (either immediate needs or more holistic needs) and work within the status quo rather than address the causes of the unjust systems that create homelessness. In *Divini Redemptoris*, Pope Pius XI wrote that while acts of charity are holy and vital, "Let no one attempt with trifling charitable donations to exempt themselves from the great duties imposed by justice." Those words still ring true today. So how could your church respond to the issue of homelessness from a justice perspective?

To begin with, we need to understand the root causes of the injustice. Without spending a chapter on this issue, we can point to some key directions. First, the majority of people experiencing homelessness in America work, and many are children. Shockingly, there is no municipality in America where a person working full-time for minimum wage can afford to rent a market-rate, two-bedroom apartment without becoming housing insecure. So the key underlying issue is a lack of affordable housing. Second, when we think about the chronically homeless, the underlying issues include lack of access to mental health care and addiction treatment as well as systemic barriers to employment, especially for people with criminal records. So a justice response must address these root causes and change the systems that create and uphold them. These efforts might include ordinances raising the minimum wage to a living wage that would allow working people to afford housing, or alternatively (or maybe additionally) the creation of vastly more affordable housing. Similarly, a justice response to chronic homelessness might include legislation for universal health care or equalizing treatment for mental illness with physical illness. Or we might organize to ensure employment opportunities for people with records or the long-term unemployed. Doing these sort of campaigns would definitely challenge the status quo and expose conflict, but they are also necessary, alongside the important charitable work, to actually end homelessness.

Does your church care about homelessness? When you choose to address it, do your efforts include options from both sides of this coin?

While I was at Community Renewal Society, we created an exercise to help churches examine their ministries. Take several pieces of butcher paper and draw a spectrum from charity on one side to justice on the other. Then take a bunch of Post-it Notes and write all the outward facing ministries that your church does, one per Post-it. You might have "food pantry" on one or "letter writing with an advocacy organization" on another. Then go up and put each post-it on the spectrum where you think it belongs, using the criteria laid out above. What would your church's spectrum look like?

There will probably be a bunch of post-its on the charity side of the spectrum, with a smaller group in the middle because they have aspects of both or include education on larger societal issues, with only a few lonely post-its on the justice end of the spectrum. Our ministries are out of balance! As a church, we invest vastly more time and energy in the works of charity than we do in the works of justice, if we do any justice at all. Despite Pope Pius's admonition, we do attempt to use our work of charity to exempt ourselves from the great duties imposed by justice.

Why is this the case? Why are we so hesitant to engage the work of justice, despite the clear gospel mandate to do so?

I think there are two key reasons. The first is that we just don't know how. Feeding someone who is hungry seems straightforward enough, but changing the economics of the food industry? How do we even start!? Hopefully, the rest of this book can offer some answers to those questions.

But the second key reason goes back to the question of the status quo. As long as you remain in the charitable lane, very few people will criticize you, and there will be very little conflict—"when I give food to the poor, they call me a saint," but if you begin to engage the powers and principalities and confront issues of justice, tensions will arise—"when I ask why the poor have no food, they call me a communist." And one of the first critiques that will be raised is that you are being "political" and that the church isn't supposed to be engaged in "politics."

So can churches be political?

The first question is, what do we mean by "politics"? And here, I think it is useful to make a distinction between being political and being partisan, because we often confuse the two. To be partisan, in the American democratic tradition, is to advocate for a certain party or candidate, and that is something the church definitely should not do: first, because there is no candidate, party, or platform that perfectly conforms to God's vision for the kingdom; and, second, because your church can lose its tax-exempt status.

But if we cannot be partisan and endorse candidates, does that mean we cannot be political? A great deal of our understanding of the idea of politics and political science comes from early Greek philosophy, specifically from Aristotle and his treatise aptly named *Politics*. That title literally translates as "on things concerning the polis." The *polis* in turn means the political community or the city-state. So politics is about seeking the optimum welfare of the people within the city-state (or in our case, country or world). To put it another way that we may be more familiar with, "seek the welfare of the city" (Jeremiah 29:7). So politics is about seeking the proper administration of our governing structures and distribution of our resources and public goods.

Let's go back to Jesus's mission statement in Luke 4:18-19 again. We are called to bring good news to the poor, end oppression, release prisoners, provide health care to the disabled, and redistribute wealth downward toward those who have the least. Jesus's message is inherently political, which is one of the key reasons he was vilified and ultimately crucified by the Roman government and by elements of the Jewish leadership whom they had coopted. In fact, crucifixion itself was a political penalty, not meant for mere criminals but for those who opposed the authority of Rome. The gospel message, and the prophetic tradition that Jesus stood in, is a call for political change, and a far more radical one than is heard from any mainstream political party or candidate.

So not only can the church be political, but we must be. Without engaging in the decision-making process of our society, we cannot fulfill all aspects of Jesus's call to us to act on behalf of the least in our society with both charity and justice, and to challenge any law or structure that does not pass God's test of first and foremost caring for those on the margins. God has anointed us all, as followers of Jesus, to be agents of good news for the poor, the oppressed, the orphan, the widow, and the immigrant.

Are you ready to follow Jesus's call to build God's kingdom with both hands, charity and justice?

Are you and your church ready to become "political" for the sake of gospel justice?

CHAPTER 2

For God Has Not Given Us a Spirit of Fear, but of Power

Three teenagers walk down 127th Street in Harlem on a summer afternoon. As adolescents, we walk with a swagger, attempting to convey the toughness we've seen in older men and begun to learn in the streets. Our baggy pants swish as we walk. A police car comes around the corner. Fast. With lights flashing and the siren blaring, it screeches to a stop right behind us. Two cops, both white, get out with their guns drawn. "Show me your hands!" Six hands go up. The officers approach. Each one grabs one of my friends and shoves him onto the hood of the car. Somehow, I'm almost invisible. One of the cops mutters something to me about backing away as they toss my friends. I take a step back, always amazed at how calmly they handle being grabbed, shoved, threatened, poked, and prodded by men with guns. Even as a teenager, I knew that my white skin protected me from that kind of treatment.

In this particular instance, nothing else drastic happened. After patting my friends down and issuing some warnings about going home and staying out of trouble, the cops drove off without a word of apology or any attempt at reconciliation. We laughed and joked with one another as we went our way.

Looking back, I can recognize three distinct emotions running through me in that moment. The first was a mocking vindication;

you see, I was carrying the drugs. We had a little weed on us, but we already knew that you should always have the white kid carry the contraband. People who looked like me weren't the ones who had to worry about police harassment during the stop-and-frisk years in New York City. Like any teenager putting something over on adult authority, I wanted to jeer and laugh.

The second, because every teenage boy wants to be perceived as tough, was a feeling of offense: "What!? I don't look bad?" I had been in my fair share of fights and scrapes by that point, and wanted to be known as someone you don't mess with. I could rap along with "F*#K tha Police" and the Notorious B.I.G. How dare they not see what a bad "motha'" I was? They should have had *me* up against that car!

But hidden behind all that was a feeling I didn't recognize until much later. I was ashamed. Ashamed that my friends were being violated and assaulted, while I was spared, based solely on the color of our skin. And I was angry, not just at the officers but about something deeper. I was angry at myself, angry at the world, angry that I couldn't *do* anything in that moment. All I could do was stand back and watch this violation happen. I was powerless in the face of injustice. I didn't have any tools to stop or change it, and, because of the color of my skin, I couldn't even endure the experience myself. I wanted to do more than bear silent witness to this injustice. I wanted to change it!

Do you remember feeling powerless? Helpless to make a change that you know needed to happen, or defend someone from being wronged?

In those moments of powerlessness, God may speak to us and call us to action and transformation.

Years later, as an organizer, I find myself standing in a church basement, with twenty or thirty members of several local congregations sitting at folding tables arranged in an open U-shape.

"Stand up if this sentence describes you: I am power hungry!"

Only three people tentatively stand up.

There's nothing surprising about this. Most of us associate people who are power hungry with oppressors—big, heartless corporations or craven politicians, who step on the little guy for their own personal gain or career advancement. So most of us, when asked this question, stay seated.

"All right, stand up if this sentence describes you: I am justice hungry!"

The whole room springs to their feet. This is a justice training session, after all. Who doesn't hunger and thirst for justice and righteousness? After all, Jesus blessed the justice hungry in his Sermon on the Mount! If you are reading this book, I'm sure that you would be standing too.

But next I ask the three people who stood up first, identifying themselves as power hungry, to sit, leaving the rest of the room standing. These folks have claimed to be hungry for justice, but not hungry for power. And then I'm forced to look at them and say some harsh words: "I don't believe you."

This isn't because I'm an untrusting cynic. And I'm not just trying to be a jerk or get a rise out of people. But this is simply too important an issue to let people off the hook. And if you are one of those people who would be standing, it's important for you to not let yourself off the hook either.

Dr. King (drawing deeply on the theologian Reinhold Niebuhr) wrote, "Power without love is reckless and abusive, and love without power is sentimental and anemic." We cannot claim to have love for our fellow human beings, or to want to stand for justice, while refusing to seek the means by which we can actually achieve justice. This is the lesson I learned on that street corner in Harlem: to really make change, we have to move from being activists—lone voices in the wilderness who speak eloquently, read all the right books, and have a great analysis while being unable to make anything happen—to becoming powerful.

So what is it about power that makes us so uncomfortable?

When you hear the word "power," what comes to your mind?

For many people, it is the old saying, "Power corrupts and absolute power corrupts absolutely." Almost everyone has heard that power corrupts, and, even if we don't remember it, this message has sunk in. It helps explain our unwillingness to identify ourselves as power hungry. Why would you be hungry for something that will corrupt you? What kind of person are you? For most of us, when asked if power is good or bad, our gut tells us that power is something bad, a temptation to sin, an instrument of injustice.

Let's be more specific and demystify the idea of power. Instead of a vague, amorphous concept, picture something solid and tangible.

Picture an axe. Is an axe good or is it bad?

The answer is obvious; it depends on how you use it.

In fact, an axe cannot be good or bad. An axe has no moral value whatsoever; it is a piece of metal attached to a piece of wood. Now if some villain out of a horror movie comes charging toward you, bloody axe raised, you would probably say that the axe is terrible. But conversely, if your house was on fire and a firefighter used the axe to break down the door and pull your children to safety, you would probably think that the axe was the greatest thing that ever existed.

Of course, in both instances, the axe itself did nothing. It was a tool held by a person. What was good or bad were the values of the person wielding the axe. And it is the same with power. Power is a tool that is neither intrinsically good nor bad. When we say that power is bad, what we are really saying is that the values for which we have seen power wielded go against our understanding of God's will for the world.

So if power is just a tool with no inherent value, good or bad, why spend so much time discussing it, especially since the concept seems to be so troubling? Dr. King's previously cited comment might offer some clues. Dr. King says that even love, the thing St. Paul called the greatest thing in the world, is sentimental and anemic without power. Power is not just a tool, it is *the* tool.

So what is power?

Simply put,

Power is the ability to act.
The ability to create, control or prevent change.

Let that sink in.

Power is the ability to make something happen, stop something from happening, or control the way that something happens. I want to create an economy that provides dignity for all people. But without the ability to actually impact the structures that create our economy of vast inequality and high levels of poverty, that wish is just a pretty dream. I want to stop the current push to hunt down, incarcerate, demonize, and deport undocumented people in America, but without the power to impact our political system that shapes immigration policy, that desire is nothing but a sad sigh in the wind. Without the ability to act to create, control, or prevent change, all our love for our fellow people, all our compassion for the downtrodden, and all our zeal for gospel justice are just another set of pretty ideas that float away.

So if power is the ability to act, how do we get it? What are the key ingredients of power? What seems to give people a lot of ability to influence our world?

The most obvious answer is money. It's sad but true. In 2019, nearly 40 percent of the members of Congress were millionaires! It costs nearly $2 million to run for Congress and over $10 million to run for the Senate, and that doesn't even count the millions and millions poured in by outside interests and donors.

So the people who can write checks big enough to put a dent in those goals exert an outsize influence on decision making in our country. Put simply, organized money is a key source of power.

But it isn't the only one. Even with all the money in the world, politicians still need to get thousands or millions of people to vote for them, and thousands more to volunteer to knock on doors and make phone calls. Masses of people and protesters have changed laws and overturned governments. Power also comes from organized people.

Power, the ability to act, comes from organized people and organized money. In fact, every significant change that has happened in the world, be it for good or bad, has been driven by a group of people organizing people and money to advance their values. And Jesus moved the same way.

Imagine this: you are at church on Sunday during worship and a shabbily dressed man marches down the center aisle right to the front of the church and upends the altar, sending the bread and wine, the chalice, the offering plates, and everything else crashing across the floor of the sanctuary. What would happen next? Almost immediately, in a polite church, the ushers or deacons would firmly pull that man off the altar and out of the sanctuary. In a less polite church, he might get tackled!

But that's exactly what Jesus does in the cleansing of the temple, and yet no one tackles him. The Jewish elders and Roman leaders, with all the military and legal might of the state behind them, can do nothing; and so, after overturning the tables, Jesus stays right there and speaks and preaches for several chapters of the Gospel! Have you ever noticed that? Why wasn't he arrested immediately?

Most of us know both the story of the cleansing of the temple and some of Jesus's teachings during it by heart, and yet, it wasn't until I began organizing that I asked why he wasn't arrested or thrown out. Then I realized the answer is right there in the text: "The chief priests and the scribes came to hear of it and were seeking to put him to death, yet they feared him because the whole crowd was amazed by his teaching" (Mark 11:18). Jesus organized a huge protest! He organized so many people behind him and his powerful vision for the arrival of God's kingdom that even the rulers of the land cannot arrest him in their own temple.

We so often perceive Jesus as having been hated by the crowds, but a careful reading of the Gospel tells us something else. If Jesus had been hated by the masses, if he had not organized an incredibly powerful base of people to march on Jerusalem with him, the authorities could have arrested him at any time. We see in the Gospel story a few chapters later, "The chief priests and the scribes were seeking a way to arrest him by treachery and put him to death. They said, 'Not during the festival, for fear that there may be a riot among the people'" (Mark 14:1-2). Generally, arresting someone with few followers and little power does not cause a riot. Instead, the chief priests need to get inside information. They only need Judas to betray Jesus because they know they have to find him when he is alone, away from his large crowd of followers, and then they need to convince Pilate to execute him before the people find out! That's why they arrest Jesus during the preparation day for the Passover, when all the Jews are at home and busy. Jesus makes this point himself when he is arrested, "Day after day I was with you in the temple area and you did not seize me" (Luke 22:53).

When we think of other leaders, we can find the same thing. We all know the "I Have a Dream" speech that Dr. King delivered, but why is that speech so famous? It may not have been one of his best. It wasn't even particularly original material (much of it was recycled from his many addresses). But it was given at the largest political demonstration in American history up to that point—the March on Washington. A quarter of a million people had descended on the nation's capital that day for jobs and freedom. Those numbers had never been seen before, and that many organized people, that much power, could not be ignored.

At the same time, many of King's other best-known addresses were in large, upscale Northern churches. What was he doing there? He was certainly building support for his Southern movement in the more progressive North, but, more concretely, he was fund-raising. Paying a staff, renting offices, bussing people to demonstrations, and bailing people out of jail all cost money, and King knew that to build a movement, even one whose main power would come from organized people, he had to organize money too.

So if we want to actually achieve change, if we want our fire for justice to be more than a candle in the wind, we have to get serious about building and using power. We have to, with focus and intentionality, organize people and organize money around the core values of our faith to help build the kingdom of God.

One pastor who struggled with, and then embraced, this concept during our work together is Rev. Alan Taylor, the pastor of Unity Temple in Oak Park, Illinois. He shared his story with me:

I was in my thirteenth year of ministry, and my eighth year at Unity Temple. I had long wanted to engage public ministry and pursue social justice, but I didn't know how to begin. I had figured out how to grow a mission-focused congregation. I had developed a strong staff and cultivated many leaders. I led a congregation highly respected in our denomination and wider community. We had a lot going for us except we were woefully ineffective when it came to working for justice.

The turning point was my participation in a three-day organizing training. During this training, I had several "aha" experiences. First, when hearing how Martin Luther King Jr. viewed power, I was drawn in. Here was an articulation of how I believe deep down we religious leaders should move through the world. We should claim our authority as moral leaders rather than shirk it as I and so many others have been accustomed to doing in the  *name of being congenial. I needed to claim my authority both as a human being and an ordained religious leader. I needed a healthier ego—a willingness to say "This is what's important to me and my people" to those who have the power to change the world. I needed to claim my capacity to stand as a leader in my community. I needed to live into the reality that my leadership comes not from being liked but being respected.*

I also came to appreciate the difference between personal and professional relationships. And I realized: in our public relationships, like those with elected officials, we don't persuade people because they like us but because they respect us. I had never sought to cultivate an "activist congregation," but with the training it became clear that I wanted to cultivate a "powerful congregation": a congregation with the capacity to influence people who have the power to make key decisions.

I was uncomfortable the first time I entered a meeting with my state senator. We were there to express discontent with the lack of response among legislators to address the challenges of people with criminal records. It felt so unnatural to create tension by expressing our frustration with the lack of action and to make clear demands instead of nice sounding requests. It seemed to go against my grain as a warm, thoughtful religious leader. But our honesty and clarity, coupled with the fact that our demands were backed up by the power of our entire congregation, elicited an honest reaction from the senator. We came with two specific asks—to become the lead sponsor of a bill to seal the records of felons convicted of nonviolent crimes and to attend the Martin

Luther King Faith in Action Assembly and publicly express his support. Over the course of the meeting, he agreed.

My congregation learned the techniques of faith-based organizing and turned out over a hundred people to some actions—and our local state representatives and senators took note. After one such action, that same senator, now an ally impressed with our power, told me to get people to Springfield. I brought thirty people who boarded a bus at 6 a.m. on a work day and joined three hundred other members of other churches. We learned that our members knew how to talk with Republicans—and got two to sign on that day. Today the bill is the law in Illinois.

When one of our representatives was on the fence about marriage equality, I was asked if I could get twenty-five people out to an action at his office on a work day. Over thirty people from Unity Temple joined the group of just over one hundred—and within two days, he became the sixtieth vote that passed this legislation.

I still have a gentle, pastoral presence, coupled with a quiet firm dignity. When I am clear what I want from an encounter with a power broker, I don't need to be an alpha male or a supersmart person, but instead I need to bring my own quiet presence as a human being who has organized a large number of people actively engaged in promoting the common good. It still is surprising to me to witness how powerful individuals will respond to my simple yet direct requests.

Reverend Taylor learned that, if he didn't embrace the need for power, he couldn't be the leader and pastor he wanted to be, and his church couldn't be the church it wanted to be. His congregation was full of activists, and the congregation made statements about all the issues. All his convictions didn't produce any results until he got serious about power. But even with all of that, many of us are still wary of the idea of building power or being power hungry. We return again and again to the idea that power will, in some way, corrupt us.

So let's go back to that famous quote for a second: "Power corrupts and absolute power corrupts absolutely." You have heard that quote a hundred times, I'll bet. In fact, it's become a catchphrase in our society, repeated in TV dramas and morality plays. Here's a quick quiz then, since this common knowledge has spread so far. Who originally said it?

I bet you answered Machiavelli, didn't you? It sounds "Machiavellian," even if we don't know a lot about who Machiavelli was. Maybe you think it's a quote from the Bible or a saying from a famous Buddhist text. In fact, it is from none of these sources. The source of this famous statement is a nineteenth-century English Catholic historian John Lord Acton, and I'll bet you dollars to doughnuts that you've never heard of him, or if you have, all you know about him is this famous quote!

And here's another interesting fact. You know how you have heard that quote over and over again throughout your life? Well, you've been hearing it wrong! And so have I. And so has everyone else. The actual quote is, "Power *tends* to corrupt and absolute power corrupts absolutely." Ask one hundred people about this quote, and I guarantee they will all get it wrong in exactly the same way.

Isn't it amazing what a difference a word makes? By eliminating the word "tends" we have removed any ambiguity about power; to have it is to be corrupted. Anyone who wants to be a force for good in the world must avoid it at all costs!

But what happens when we avoid power?

Let's return to our metaphor of the axe for a moment. I don't know about you, but I know that I have skipped way too many days at the gym to break down the doors of burning buildings without an axe, meaning that, if I don't have one, I can't get in to rescue my children. Even worse, if I don't pick up the axe, if I leave it sitting on the table, what will happen?

Someone else is going to come and pick it up! And that person may not share our values. In fact, the likelihood is that they won't. The type of people who are totally comfortable hacking down anyone who gets in their way are almost always happy to pick up the axe, and they are even more thrilled if we refuse to do so: Hey! More axes for them and less resistance standing in their way!

But if we pick up the axe, like Pastor Taylor, we discover that having power can be fun! We don't have to wield it the way other people have. Instead of hoarding the axe for ourselves, using it to threaten people and benefit only a few of our cronies, we can use it as a creative tool to save us and build for the common good. We can use the axe to build more opportunities for other people, and even train our allies on how to use an axe and create one for themselves.

All well and good, but in the real world, we aren't talking about burning babies or attacks from axe-wielding maniacs, right?

Well, in America today, perhaps the richest and most powerful country the world has ever seen, one in five children goes to bed hungry every night. One in three African American men will be under the control of the criminal justice system at some point in their lives. A 2011 study found that, in America, approximately 245,000 deaths in the United States in 2000 were attributable to low education, 176,000 to racial segregation, 162,000 to low social support, 133,000 to individual-level poverty, 119,000 to income inequality, and 39,000 to area-level poverty. Every twenty-eight hours a black person is killed by a police officer, security guard, or vigilante.

Think about how amazing it would feel to actually pick up the axe, to be able to affect and change these injustices! When I was standing on that street in Harlem, watching my friends get harassed, I was experiencing the awful pain and impotence of being powerless in the face of injustice. It was later on, as I grew and reflected, that I realized that, in that moment, what I needed, what my friends needed, and what our community needed was the power to control our own lives, our own bodies, and our own destinies.

It turns out that it is a life-or-death question after all.

In Matthew 25, Jesus tells his disciples about the last judgment, how people will be sorted and judged because "whatsoever you did to the least of my people, that you did unto me." In other words, people are saved because of their acts of mercy, charity, and justice toward the least of these. But why are people sent "into the eternal fire prepared for the devil and his angels" (Matthew 25:41)? It isn't because these people took away food or drink, or put him in prison, or threw him out into the street naked. They simply refused to use their power to interrupt these conditions. Jesus tells them, "Amen, I say to you, what you did not do for the least of my people, you did not do it for me" (Matthew 25:45).

Right now, systems of destruction are creating death, hunger, imprisonment, and homelessness among the least of God's people. The axe is sitting on the table.

I can imagine Jesus saying, "Whenever you refused to do everything you could to defend the least of my people from injustice, you refused to defend me."

Do you pick up the axe?

Are you ready to become power hungry?

PART II

Preparing Our Churches:
Building Congregational Power

PART

Preparing the Churches:
Socializing and Legitimation of Power

Chapter 3

From *Power Over* to *Power With*

I had been organizing for a few years, first in Tennessee and then in Chicago. I had learned a lot of the basics, had a pretty good grasp of justice, and was serious about building power. I was already getting noticed and invited to preach, speak, and provide trainings at different churches. Some of our campaigns had already had some victories. I was serious about organizing, brash and pushy, and always ready to challenge people who weren't willing to take direct action. I had developed a gift for power analysis and understanding campaign strategy, and I was excited to be using it to put my faith into action for justice.

At Community Renewal Society, I had the honor of working under the direction of the Rev. Dr. Calvin Morris. He is a wise man, more than twice my age, who had served on Dr. King's staff and worked with Rev. Jesse Jackson to form Operation Breadbasket (later Rainbow/PUSH). He served on the boards of directors of half the justice organizations in the city and was constantly speaking and preaching. Yet he was willing to invest in a cocky twenty-something-year-old kid, offering me guidance and support.

One day, Dr. Morris called me into his office to meet. The walls were covered with awards he had won and pictures of him with luminaries of the civil rights movement and social justice icons. I sat opposite him in a large, comfortable armchair.

Dr. Morris has a very gentle pastoral presence, and he tends to ease into conversations.

"Alex, back in the days of the movement, we had a saying about people," he started. "We used to say we wanted to work with a GWM, a Good White Man."

I wasn't sure where Dr. Morris was going here, but I was always excited to hear about the movement.

"We used to say, there weren't very many GWMs around," Dr. Morris continued, "so when we found one, it was a good day."

Now, I was leaning forward, starting to feel proud of being singled out for my commitment to justice by such a revered leader. Then he looked me straight in my eye.

"You, Alex," he said to me, "are not a Good White Man. You could be, but, right now, you are not."

Dr. Morris's words hit me like a punch to the gut. How could he say that? I was working sixty hours a week to organize churches for justice! I was fighting tooth and nail to win important victories for our members! I even lived in a black community and worshiped in a black church!

On the other hand, how could I argue with the man who had been the executive director of the King Center for Nonviolence at the personal request of Coretta Scott King? A man who had forgotten more about fighting for social justice than I would ever know? A man who had poured into me and invested in my development as an organizer and as a Christian? I sat in silence, stewing away.

"You aren't a GWM because your ego is getting in your way," Dr. Morris continued. "You are so focused on being right, and on what you know about organizing that, instead of building people up, you are knocking them down. If you are going to become a GWM, you are going to have to be in better relationship with people."

It was a painful conversation. And I didn't handle it very

gracefully. I stammered something about hearing what he was saying and that I would think about it, but inside, I was seething, denying the truth Dr. Morris had spoken. It wasn't until later on that night, when I'd calmed down and gotten my ego in check a little, that I realized that he was telling me something I needed to hear. If I wanted to create power for change by organizing people, I had to focus on building relationships.

Historically, when human beings organize people for power, we do it through three ways: guns, butter, and magic. No, I haven't gone off the deep end, let me explain.

Guns. The use of force. Probably the most basic method of organizing people that we can think of. We build power by intimidating or hurting others. If you put a gun to my head, you could probably get me to do most things you wanted. In Jesus's time, the Roman Empire had "organized" the Jewish people through its military power. And we still maintain power in many situations around the world like this today.

Butter. Material benefits, or greasing the wheels. I had already learned that the Chicago machine was expert at this. For decades, it built its power through patronage. If you could get one hundred of your neighbors to turn out and vote the machine line, you could be rewarded by getting on the city payroll, and get a nice check and pension even if you weren't qualified for the job or rarely showed up to work.

Magic. This one might seem the oddest. But "magic" is the way cults organize people, or, in our worst examples, the way religion has organized people. We call on an unseen power that only a few people are allowed to have access to and manipulate people's beliefs through illusions of miracles to bring them to support us. On a less drastic level, this is how highly charismatic figures can organize people. In some ways, this is what I had been trying to do, organize people through my own dazzling charisma and special knowledge.

After Jesus is baptized, he sees the Holy Spirit descending on him and hears God declare him God's "beloved son"; he goes out into the desert before beginning his public ministry. And after fasting for forty days, he is tempted by the devil (Luke 4). Have you ever noticed what the devil's temptations are?

First, "The devil said to him, 'If you are the Son of God, command this stone to become bread'" (Luke 4:3). In other words, feed people; give them something. Jesus was hungry himself, so he could appreciate how much this kind of organizing can work. If Jesus used his power to continually provide "butter," he could organize people to follow him. But Jesus refused.

Second, "the devil took him up and showed him all the kingdoms of the world in a moment of time" (Luke 4:5) and offers them to Jesus if Jesus will worship him. Again, in Jesus's time, kingdoms were created and supported by armies and soldiers. Monarchs maintained their power through force, so what the devil was really offering was the power of guns. And once again, Jesus refused.

Finally, "he took him to Jerusalem and set him on the pinnacle of the temple and said to him, 'If you are the Son of God, throw yourself down from here, for it is written, "He will command his angels concerning you, to guard you," and "On their hands they will bear you up, lest you strike your foot against a stone"'" (Luke 4:9-11). In other words, jump off the roof of the highest building in the city and fly—perform a magic trick! That would *definitely* get people's attention, and I'll bet they would follow you. Of course Jesus says no to this final temptation as well and begins his public ministry using different tools.

What different tools?

Jesus shows us there is a fourth way to organize people, and it is the complete opposite, philosophically and morally, of the other three. We can build mutual, public relationships and have power *with* others. Unlike guns, butter, and magic, where all the control lies with one party, relationships have to be based on mutual respect and concern. If I'm organizing people only to benefit me and organizing them with guns, butter, or magic, there isn't a lot that those people can do about it: deal with it or become the victim of the gun; lose access to the butter; or be denied the magic. So people power based on guns, butter, or magic is easily abused. But that's a lot harder to do when your power is based on mutual relationships. Once I start using this power to benefit only myself instead of our common goals, there is nothing to hold people to me, and my power will diminish. So building power through relationships holds those who wield the power accountable to working for the common good.

When we focus on building power with others, we make relationships our number one priority. We have one-on-one conversations, ask deep questions of each other, and share our stories. We focus on building people as much as we do on winning campaigns. Our relationships are our key currency, the source of our information, our accountability mechanisms, and the fuel that keeps us going.

It was summed up for me by an old saying: Tell me who you stand with, and I'll tell you who you are. Whom we choose to be in relationship with, and whom we invest in and take risks for, those relationships define who we are. Our relationships are a public manifestation of our values.

You say you believe in empowering people? Who are the leaders you have been developing?

You say that you believe in combatting racism? What people of color have you made yourself accountable to through intentional relationship building?

You say you believe in grass-roots power? How do you spend your time really getting to know local residents in your community?

Following Dr. Morris's challenge, I began to focus on how I was doing this and who I was doing it with. I let my issue research take a back seat for a few weeks, and I spent time in one-on-one conversations with a number of our members whom I had only engaged with in strategy sessions before. I learned about them, and what brought them to the work. Sure, maybe they didn't know as much about organizing as I did, but these were seniors who had decades of lived experience and had knowledge about their communities and churches that was deeper than historical records. They knew how to get things moving; they knew who to avoid, and they knew what was really important for them and their neighbors.

As I thought about how to develop leaders, I stopped writing and sending out agendas for strategy meetings myself, or with one other staff person. Instead, I held several conversations with different members before the meetings to talk about what we thought the goals would be. Then we sat down with the member who was going to serve as the meeting chair, and we wrote the agenda together. If we felt that there were key concepts or skills that would be needed, I would provide a short training for everyone at the beginning of the meeting. And I made a rule for myself to never present an idea to start a discussion; I had to ask a question instead. I asked one wonderfully cantankerous leader to hold me accountable to this. If I started spouting off, she would look at me across the table and say, "Alright, kiddo, that's enough out of you!" It was the perfect way to make sure I didn't take myself too seriously (and she and the other leaders loved it).

I would still challenge people, pushing them to grow, or urging them to see a better strategic move, but now, instead of bulldozing whomever I felt like, I was talking with people with whom I had relationships. And they could hear me and listen to my challenge because they could trust that I actually cared about them. They weren't pawns in *my* power-building scheme; we were partners building power together for our shared vision.

But even as I made this shift, I was still learning. "Relationship" can be a confusing word. As we focus on building relational power in our churches and communities, it is important to make a distinction between public and private relationships, because our public relationships have a very different quality than our private relationships, and confusing the two can be one of the biggest hurdles in building congregational power to fight for justice.

So what's the difference?

First of all, the goals of the relationships are different. Our private relationships' goals are to be liked, while our public relationships' goals are to advance our vision for the world. Our private relationships are based on shared interests, while our public relationships are based on shared values. The key components of our private relationships are unconditional love and fun experiences, while the key components of our public relationship are mutual accountability and respect.

As a born and raised New Yorker, I'm a dyed-in-the-wool Yankees fan (I know, I know, the evil empire, but I came to love them in the late '80s and early '90s when they were bad!). If you cut me, I bleed Yankee pinstripes; and my father likes to ruefully say that I learned half my vocabulary in the bleachers of Yankee Stadium. So I find it really hard to have private relationships with Red Sox fans. Our inbred loathing is too deep. And at the end of a long week when I want to kick back and watch a baseball game or talk sports, a Bostonian is just not the person I'm going to call!

But this doesn't mean I can't have meaningful, public relationships with Bostonians! We can share faith values, identify issues of mutual concern, and organize together for justice.

Why is this distinction so important? Because when we are unclear about what kind of relationships we are building, people get confused. I learned this lesson the hard way when I met a young woman among a group of grad students who I thought might be a fantastic new leader of our organization. So I asked her to meet up for a one-on-one.

Or so I thought.

"Hey could we meet up for a cup of coffee sometime next week?" I asked. "I would love to get to know you better and learn more about you and why you care about social justice."

So we agreed on a place and time. We met up and started talking. After a few minutes it slowly began to dawn on me: I thought we were in a one-on-one, and she thought we were on a date! Needless to say, it did not go well. It was embarrassing and awkward, and, perhaps even more to the point, she did not get a new boyfriend, and I did not recruit a new leader for our organization. We both left disappointed.

What on earth happened here?

I had not been clear with her about my goals and what kind of a relationship I was trying to build. Looking back now, it's a funny, egg-on-my-face story, but it was also a lesson I had to learn about what goes wrong when we are not clear about the kind of relationship we are building.

But public does not mean shallow or impersonal. In fact, bringing clear intentionality to a public relationship leads to very deep conversation and connection. I have had one-on-ones where people tell me about being victims of abuse or sexual assault, watching their children struggle with incarceration or drug addiction, losing a loved one to violence, or their most personal moments of prayer and engagement with God. And in turn, I've shared stories from my own life of fear, violence, and loss. In fact, it is only by really understanding what a person cares about and values, what their vision is for the world and their role in it, and their own story and testimony, that we can have the kind of relationships that allow us to move into action together, challenge one another with love, and stick together through tough times and sometimes demoralizing campaigns.

The movement from *power over* to *power with* means we have to shift the way we think about justice work and power building. We need to move away from talking at people about issues, to talking with people about their stories, values, anger, and dreams. We need to spend less time on speeches, educational forums, and perfecting treatises and more on developing the skills and abilities of the people in our churches and communities to become leaders for action.

Building shared, relational power is sometimes not flashy work. We would all like to be that person who knows the ins and outs of every issue, or who is leading the march or preaching the fiery sermon; but, if we want people to be on that march, or we want our knowledge to actually lead to change, we instead need to focus on building long-term public relationships and structures in our churches. Rather than read another book or hold another issue forum, we need instead to focus on authentically relating to, moving with, and developing others.

Are you ready to stop talking at people about issues and start talking with people to build relationships?

CHAPTER 4

What Do You Want Me to Do for You?

Listen

Has this ever happened to you or your church? You see an issue in your neighborhood or hear about something on the news. You immediately feel deeply compelled to do something. Maybe you want to start a program to support struggling families. Maybe you want to begin a feeding ministry. Maybe you want to tutor or educate children or young adults. The need is clear.

So you check in with your church. You talk with your pastor and maybe present an idea to the church council for a program or workshop. They tell you, "Sure, if you want to do it, go for it." So you plan an impressive event or series of events. You work hard developing the presentation or curriculum, really educating yourself, even recruiting high-quality speakers or materials. You make nice flyers and share the event all over social media.

But, then something odd happens. The same people from your church or circle who come to everything show up, but few others do. Even more disappointing, very few of the actual people that your ministry was meant to serve attend, even though you are sure that what you are offering would benefit them.

The next meeting has even fewer folks, and eventually your effort peters out. You are left demoralized. You might even hear comments like, "People around here don't even want to help themselves" or "our church just doesn't care about anything."

Early in my career, my organization decided to host a faith summit on criminal justice reform. Recognizing how damaging the criminal justice system was, particularly to people of color, our goal was to convene dozens of organizations and thousands of people of faith together to launch a movement around a new vision and set of principles for criminal justice. And it was a beautiful platform: treatment and diversion for those suffering from addiction and mental illness, focusing incarceration on rehabilitation instead of punishment, removing barriers to successful reentry, caring for the families of people touched by the system, and healing for victims of crime and violence.

But there was one problem. (Okay, there were many problems, but let's just focus on the biggest one); almost all the planning was done by the small, mostly (at that time) white, staff of our organization. No one directly touched by mass incarceration was in the inner circle. Instead, we simply laid out a platform and a vision and asked people to show up.

They didn't.

On the day of the summit, the forum that could hold almost two thousand people had just a few hundred. We looked out at whole sections of seats that were completely empty. What's worse, at least one hundred of the people who did come were simply representing other organizations that were talking about their own work. There were some powerful speakers, but, as a whole, the summit was a big disappointment for me, and, I'm sad to say, did not launch a new movement of people of faith to transform the criminal justice system.

I've seen this general story play out over and over, whether it is a revival to talk about justice issues or a new community-service ministry. While some efforts are more successful than others, this outline holds true a lot of the time. So what is going on here?

After repeating this pattern over and over, it's time to accept that there is a problem with the way we approach and plan this work. There is another way, and the scriptures offer us guidance.

Remember the story of blind Bartimaeus? It's really famous, but there are some often overlooked kernels of learning for us today. You can read the story in all three of the Synoptic Gospels, Mark 10:46-52, Matthew 20:29-34, or Luke 18:35-43:

> Then they came to Jericho. As Jesus and his disciples, together with a large crowd, were leaving the city, a blind man, Bartimaeus (which means "son of Timaeus"), was sitting by the roadside begging. When he heard that it was Jesus of Nazareth, he began to shout, "Jesus, Son of David, have mercy on me!"
>
> Many rebuked him and told him to be quiet, but he shouted all the more, "Son of David, have mercy on me!"
>
> Jesus stopped and said, "Call him."
>
> So they called to the blind man, "Cheer up! On your feet! He's calling you." Throwing his cloak aside, he jumped to his feet and came to Jesus.
>
> "What do you want me to do for you?" Jesus asked him.
>
> The blind man said, "Rabbi, I want to see."
>
> "Go," said Jesus, "your faith has healed you." Immediately he received his sight and followed Jesus on the way. (Mark 10:46-52)

Now many commentaries and sermons on this scripture focus on two elements, God's ability to heal us from anything and the fact that nothing should stop us or dissuade us from calling out to Jesus. But something else always strikes me here. Jesus encounters this man, calling out to him for help. Bartimaeus has an obvious disability, and Jesus is God incarnate, all-knowing and all-powerful. And yet, Jesus stops and asks: "What do you want me to do for you?" He allows Bartimaeus to name the change that he wants to see.

What a radical idea! What, on the surface, seems like a simple question actually holds a far more profound and transformational message about how we should be approaching ministry and justice work. God knows our hearts and our deepest desires, and yet Jesus does not simply heal Bartimaeus. He asks him what change he wants to see. But we, on the other hand, without divine knowledge and judgment, are often very ready to say what is best for other people without even talking to them.

Moreover, Jesus's healing is not a one-way act. He engages Bartimaeus in the transformation ("your faith has healed you") and then in his ministry itself. Bartimaeus "follows him on the way," which leads immediately into Jerusalem to confront the Romans and the Jewish leaders. Jesus does not see this beggar as a passive recipient of his healing. In God's eyes, he is a full person, created to participate in his own liberation, first from his physical blindness and then in confronting the powers that oppress him and so many others in his community.

Growing up on the border of Spanish Harlem and Harlem at a time when Harlem was known as the poster example of urban poverty, crime and blight, there was always a lot of discussion about how to "fix" the neighborhood on TV from elected officials and even civic and business leaders. Being just down the hill from Columbia University, one of the great academic institutions of our country, didn't help. It seemed like there was a parade of professors and grad students coming down the hill to propose ways to address the social ills of the neighborhood. But most often, I found that the "diagnoses" and "solutions" fell into two categories: either they simply didn't identify the real concerns on the ground, or, more regularly, the solution to a real problem (too much violence, poor performing schools, rampant drug use, etc.) simply did not fit the lived experience of people on the streets. Recently, in Chicago and around the country, I've seen similar problems. Leaders recognize that a school in a community is struggling and decide to shut it down and send kids to a "better" school a little bit farther away, without understanding that the schools are separated by a gang line and sending kids across it endangers their lives, or that the school is actually a hub for a lot of important community-building work and shutting it down will exacerbate the issues that created educational struggles in the first place.

So often, the people who are victimized by injustice are seen, even in our own churches and neighborhoods, as problems to be fixed rather than knowledgeable and powerful leaders to be cultivated. Our communities are acted upon both by well-intentioned "allies" and less-well-meaning forces. But rarely are the people who directly experience the problem, or whom we are hoping to directly engage in our work, at the heart of creating it.

Ask yourself, are your ministries led and shaped by those they are aimed to serve?

Do you have real relationships with the people you are hoping to engage in your ministry, either the members of your church that you want to join your efforts or the people in your church and community that you hope to serve?

If the answer is no, there are two key problems. First, you cannot expect to properly address an issue if you ignore the wisdom of the people most directly affected by it. And second, if we do not center the poor and oppressed in leading our work, we can very easily recreate the oppressive structures that we are seeking to tear down.

So what do we do instead?

Listen First

Much like Jesus with Bartimaeus, we need to start by listening. Don't spend meeting upon meeting designing a program, strategizing about a justice issue, or planning an event. Instead, start with a deeply intentional listening program designed to really understand what it is that your church or community wants and needs.

So many of us are so passionate about specific issues that we immediately start talking about them and planning events and campaigns to promote them. But when we do this, we miss the chance to actually build connections and power for our congregation and community. Maybe people are actually much more passionate about a different issue. Or maybe people would connect with the issue that you care about, but they don't make the connection to their own faith values; it's easy to blame them for just "not getting it," but in truth, the problem lies more deeply with us because we didn't take the time to listen to them, learn their story, and figure out where they are coming from.

Imagine how different your church would look to people if you approached them this way, instead of coming to "save their souls" or offer them a solution to a problem they don't even care about! And imagine how much more connected your congregation would feel to your social justice work if it began by really listening to what issues were affecting the lives and the hearts of your members.

Most importantly, we must listen to the voices of people directly affected by the issues we are concerned with. People of good will often want to move into action, but we need to realize that we may not actually understand an issue. Over the past several years, I have been challenged and inspired by much of the work of the Black Lives Matter movement and an organization based in Chicago, the Black Youth Project 100. This organization has a credo that I think we should all remember: "We are the experts on our own experience." In other words, young black people are the ones best equipped to understand their needs and the needs of their communities. So often the solution that looks good on paper or in a public-policy class is not what is truly needed in the streets and homes of the people most affected by an issue.

A number of years ago, a friend of mine and I both realized that we were at organizations that dealt a great deal with issues facing people with criminal records but that almost no people with records were at the table deciding what we should be doing or how our work should unfold. We began talking to a number of men and women with records. After many discussions, one-on-ones, and house meetings, a group of leaders came together to found the FORCE (Fighting to Overcome Records and Create Equality) Project—a group of people with records, organizing themselves to break down the systemic barriers that were still put before them. My dear friend Eddie Bocanegra became the first organizer of the FORCE Project, but we still had trouble moving the broader criminal justice reform community to listen to the voices of people with records. Eddie shared his memory of those times:

During my first couple of months as the organizer of the FORCE Project, I attended the meetings of a broad coalition of criminal-justice advocates. I found myself surrounded by highly educated, passionate, and caring people. Frequently these meetings took place in institutions whose work I would read about only a few years ago in my prison cell. One particular afternoon, we began our meeting as we normally would by sharing our name, organization, and what brought us to this work. There must have been

about twenty people in the room, mostly white and mostly women with advanced degrees representing large or well-established institutions. In fact, I was there only because now I was employed by a significant social justice organization. As each person shared, I was able to quickly place their story. The vast majority of them were social justice or legal advocates who had professional experience with people in the criminal justice experience but no personal experience from their own lives.

It was at this meeting that I finally had the courage to openly speak a frustration that I had been wrestling with. In all the meetings that I was a part of, no one in the room, no one at the decision-making table, was actually a survivor of the justice system. People who had never been locked up were talking about what they thought were the most important changes inside penal institutions. People who had never had to come home from prison and who lived in neighborhoods with very few returning citizens were identifying the key barriers that should be deconstructed. The only time I would hear the voice of the incarcerated would be in the form of a testimony, often before legislators, once the issue and strategy had already been decided. Was this all that we are . . . a story? A prop to support someone else's argument?

So I spoke up. I acknowledged the support and dedication to the issue of the members of the coalition, but I pushed us to think past the people at this table. How could we choose issues to work on without listening to what people with records actually wanted? How could we decide what points to negotiate away and where to hold the line without letting the people who would bear the brunt of those decisions weigh in? We needed to have people directly impacted by these issues lead the charge for the change we were advocating for.

It was at this moment that I committed myself not to have others tell my story or the story of the other FORCE members, but to let us all tell our own stories and go about bringing the change we are seeking. It wasn't an easy conversation, and I may have offended some of the people there; but, eventually, it led to the formation of a new coalition, led by people with records, who identified the most vital issues we wanted to address. We eventually passed a number of major pieces of legislation. And I went from being a token to being the organizer of a movement that looked beyond someone's story and saw a full human being and leader.

Eddie's courage challenged the way these activists approached their work. By insisting that criminal justice advocates listen to people with records and take their wisdom into account, he fundamentally changed the way a number of people and organizations moved and acted.

Who Really Decides?

Listening is hard. There is no doubt about it. Anyone who has ever had a bitter fight with a loved one knows this. It's very difficult to put aside our own sense of knowing, and even our own focused vision, to create space to let other voices in. I've always struggled with having an ego that may be too big, so learning to listen has been a tough battle for me (and I'm still far from perfect—ask my co-workers or, God forbid, my wife). There are a couple of ways that we can fool ourselves into thinking we are listening, but in fact we are still making sure we get our own way. We have to ask, in the end, who is really making decisions.

Do people really have the option to say no, to contradict me, or tell me to go to hell when I claim that I am listening? When we are approaching people we can end up selling our own ideas; and, particularly, when we are approaching poor people or people with little opportunity, we can very easily set up a dynamic where we will offer the thing that we want to do, with an unspoken message that, if this is not the path chosen, people are on their own. We need to avoid this by having real conversations that ask people in an open-ended way what changes they most want to see. And we have to be prepared to recognize that what we first thought might be wrong. To serve our greater call of being powerful change agents, we must let go of our need to always get our way or be right.

Listening has to mean going deeper than doing a survey or

getting people to say that our idea is a good one. It has to mean inviting new voices into the decision-making space. Just as Jesus asked Bartimaeus what he wanted to have happen, urged him to take some proactive steps to make the change, and then engaged him in the ongoing work of spreading the good news of justice and liberation, we must ask our churches and communities what they want. After our listening reveals the issues that are most on the minds and hearts of our congregations and communities, we need to ask those people to join us and take leadership in shaping our responses, clarifying the policies we want to change, and planning the actions and programs we want to take.

But inviting new people into leadership does not mean that we disengage. If we want to build power and new leadership, as we ask others to lead the decision making and planning, we still need to be at every meeting. Moreover, especially when we are engaging people who have never been a part of an organizing campaign before, we have to ensure that we are not setting people up for failure; we need to have training, coaching, and support in place so that people can actively participate in decision making about their churches and their lives. We also need to demand that our planning and decision-making spaces are open to new people. This means we do sometimes have to slow things down to make sure that voices are heard, and we need to avoid technocratic jargon or insider talk that excludes people with less experience or education. If all of the technical knowledge and know-how is held by a few people, we are still holding the true decision-making power in our hands.

Listening also does not mean we leave our own sense of self, our own knowledge and experience, and our belief in right and wrong at the door. Imagine if Bartimaeus, instead of asking to see, had said, "Jesus, a lot of people have bullied me and been mean to me because of my blindness, can you please strike them all blind, so they can suffer in turn?" Would Jesus have done it? I doubt it.

In the same way, we listen and allow people truly to tell us what needs to be addressed, but we also bring our own values, knowledge, and experience to the table to support the direction we hear. For example, while I will never tell people what issues they should care about, I will offer to provide training and advice from my experience on how to win an issue campaign. If a group I am working with wants to try a tactic that I have seen fail in other places, I will often share that story and ask how we can avoid making a similar mistake. St. Paul famously tells us that we are many parts but we are all one body. Listening means sometimes allowing other people to be the eyes, with the vision of where we must go, or the mouth to speak for us, but at the same time putting all our energy into being the feet, to propel our work forward, or the fingers, to ensure that the intricate details of the vision are carried out.

A Word to and about Middle-Class White People

Listening as an organizing skill and moral commitment might be most important when attempting to work across racial and economic lines. As a white person who has spent most of my life living in and organizing communities of color, I have to think a lot about how I am ensuring that my work is authentically about lifting people up, and that I am truly accountable to the people and communities I aim to serve. How do I ensure, in trying to stand with those most affected by injustice, that I am not re-creating oppressive systems or feeding my own ego? And, for people of color, who have experienced so much oppression and hurt at the hands of white people, what expectations should be set for middle-class white people to call themselves allies? What does true, gospel listening look like?

Here are a few guideposts that I've developed to check if I listening to build authentic relationship to move toward justice, or not.

Am I here to "learn" or to act?

Very often, well-intentioned people from white, suburban churches talk about wanting to learn about the lives of people living on the margins. On the face of it, this sounds like a good thing. We don't want people to be ignorant of what the lives of poor people and people of color are like. And, if middle-class, white, suburban people are going to advocate for racial and economic justice, we would not want to do so without relationship with or knowledge of those very communities.

But that can be a big "if." So often, it feels like we want to educate ourselves and stop there. And what good is our being educated really doing to someone who may be thrown out of their housing tomorrow?

Instead, listening must come with a commitment to follow up on learning with concrete action. To do otherwise is to treat people and communities of color not as people to have relationships with, respect, and move in solidarity with, but as anthropological studies for one's own edification. It is easy to enter into voyeurism or "poverty porn," simply learning to feed ourselves.

So when I ask for a one-on-one with you or to learn about your church and neighborhood, ask, "Are you also committed to taking action with me to address the issues we discuss?" If I can't answer that question with a yes, you shouldn't waste your time meeting with me; and until I can, I should stop asking people of color to spend their valuable time educating me.

Am I there to show that I am different, or will I organize my own people?

Very often, as well-intentioned white people, we can seek to be in relationship with people of color to show how different and "un-racist" we are in comparison to "those other white people." We seek out relationships with people of color maybe by attending or visiting a black or Latino church; sometimes we even move into neighborhoods of color to be in solidarity.

Again, there may not be anything wrong with these behaviors. Many are even laudable. However, they can also tend toward the old "some of my best friends are black" behaviors. Are we authentically seeking out relationships to move toward justice, or are we seeking to use people of color as props to show how enlightened we are?

I've found that a good way to test this it to ask if I am willing to use my privilege to challenge racism in others, and, if I am willing to take risks to go and organize my own people around the issues of people and communities of color. As white people, rather than spending all our time organizing in communities of color, maybe we need to be willing to organize in our own communities as well, challenging racism, and building power that can actually move in solidarity.

Black and Latino communities often need authentic allies in white communities more than another white person showing up to "support" them in theirs. And an ally brings something to the table, not just a supportive shoulder but power to help address the issues we are facing. So, if we, as white people or members of a white church, say we want to build a relationship with you as a person of color, ask us, "Are you also going to organize and build power to support our efforts and challenge racism and injustice in your own community?"

Can I accept that I don't have the answers, deal with my own discomfort, and hand over authority?
A final check for middle-class white people doing cross-cultural social justice work is to determine how far out of our comfort zone we are willing to go. God is constantly calling us to take risks, to go where we haven't gone before, and to be uncomfortable. Jesus calls Peter to walk on water and tells a young man that, to follow, he cannot even bury his dead

father; he must come now. We have to do the same and be willing to sacrifice our own comfort.

As a man, I cannot claim to know what it is like to live in this world as a woman. In this same way, as a white person, I cannot claim to know what it is like to live in America as a person of color. So the fact that a black person's experience of interacting with the police may not resonate with mine shouldn't come as a surprise. Or, in more subtle ways, I may not be offended by a comment, joke, or look. But listening means I have to acknowledge that there are perspectives different from mine, and the fact that I haven't experienced something doesn't mean it is not true. Listening means being willing to accept that I do not know. So when other people share their experience with me, do I challenge it? Or do I accept that this is in fact their reality and commit to acting in solidarity with them to help them change it? If I find myself saying things like, "Well, that isn't my experience . . ." or "I've never seen that . . ." or "Well, I interact with so-and-so or such-and-such an institution all the time and I never see a problem," then I need to check myself and recognize that I am not really listening as a person committed to justice.

And listening as a white man committed to justice means that I need to hand over decision-making authority to people directly affected. I can offer my input, if it is asked, and certainly provide my expertise, but, in the end, I must be willing to say, "It's up to you, and I am here either way." The most obvious way that I must do this is by identifying the issues that are most important. I cannot presume to tell people whose lives I do not share what they should care most about.

Going even deeper, I must also be willing to challenge myself to be uncomfortable. We, as white people, can so often shy away from expressions of anger or pain from people of color, or become immediately defensive when people share their experience of being harmed by white people. Maybe, if you are a white person, you have even started feeling defensive in reading this section. Or we may feel that an action is "too aggressive" or "too risky for us." But is this because of legitimate strategic concerns or because of our own personal discomfort? If it's the latter, we need to be willing to take a deep breath and follow Jesus into uncharted waters.

So if I, as a white person, want to move in solidarity with a person of color, ask me (and I must ask myself), "Are you willing to hand over decision-making authority and move through your own discomfort in order to truly listen and stand together for God's kingdom?"

Make Listening Your Standard Operating Procedure

We all know how it feels to be ignored. Whether it is our spouse nodding along while looking at the phone, our co-workers not acknowledging a point we are making, or our church committee being unwilling to hear a different viewpoint, it is an infuriating experience. People talk at us, or over us, or pretend to ask for our input just to shoot it down, or wait for a moment's silence to hijack the conversation to make their point. How does it feel when you aren't listened to? Do you want to continue to be in a relationship with the other person, or do you look for a way out?

If we don't listen, we can't build strong public relationships. If we don't build strong public relationships, we can't build power. And without power, we can never create change.

But we can do things differently by following Jesus's example and putting listening at the heart of our work.

Next time you feel like calling a meeting, wait until you have held one-on-one conversations with the people you are inviting.

Before starting a campaign, make sure that directly affected people are on your leadership team, or that you are in coalition with an organization or church led by directly affected people.

Never begin a new initiative without finding out if the people in your church and community actually want it.

Can you remember the last time you felt really heard? How did it feel to be respected and taken seriously? That's the way Bartimaeus was healed, and it's exactly the way we want our collaborators, team members, and allies to feel as well. Our churches and neighborhoods are full of good ideas, hard-earned wisdom, and moving stories.

Are you ready to listen to them?

Chapter 5

An Act the Size of a Mustard Seed
The One-on-One Meeting

At the core of listening and relationship building is the one-on-one meeting (also sometimes called one-on-ones or relational meetings). These simple yet profound conversations are the cornerstone of congregational organizing and power building. And they are the most certain way I know to transform your congregation. If you want to get in shape, you have to eat right and exercise. If you want to learn an instrument, you have to practice and play scales. If you want to become powerful and expand your congregation's ability to fight for justice and win, you have to do one-on-ones. And just like exercising or learning an instrument, you won't necessarily see progress immediately, but if you keep up a steady practice, you will see long-term results. I've seen this over and over again. When a church actually commits itself to a program of one-on-ones, it becomes transformed.

One church that saw this first-hand was the Unitarian Church of Evanston. When I first encountered this church, it already had a long history of activism. It had a social justice committee, posters and flyers for different organizations and campaigns up on the announcements board, and a liturgy that regularly spoke about justice issues. And yet, the leadership of the church told me, they seemed to have problems getting the church to take action together and make an impact. And that's where a lay leader named Dale Griffin, a quiet, unassuming man, came in. Dale says:

"Well, I guess I had better call someone about doing a one-on-one," I thought to myself, with some trepidation, on Sunday evening after a three-day organizing training in 2012. "I wonder how this is going to go." We had practiced one-on-ones a few times in the training, and those were meaningful conversations; but I wondered how this would be accepted in my congregation of twenty-five years. So I called, and it went much better than I feared it might.

I had ten conversations in the next two weeks, choosing people mostly for some interest in social action. The conversations ranged from interesting to inspiring, introduced me to people I didn't know, and revealed new sides and stories of people I had known for years. The conversations led to shared interests and involvement for most people, and as a result we soon had a core leadership group. Their energy, ideas, and leadership created a new and inspiring part of our social action at UCE and had ripple effects on actions and methods in many aspects of congregational life.

The first concrete affirmation, for me, of the effectiveness of this kind of organizing happened a few months later, when eighteen UCE members joined several hundred others at the annual Martin Luther King Jr. Day of Faith in Action at a large church in Chicago. The normally staid Unitarian Universalists swayed and sung with the gospel music and listened with rapt attention to the testimony of people telling their experience, things like living in fear of violence, or struggling to find a job after incarceration. They felt powerful being part of a group holding legislators pub-

licly accountable that day. Participation continued to grow, with about thirty-five attending the MLK Day event the following year, and about seventy people the year after, and has grown or held steady each year since.

The concept of one-on-one intentional conversations spread to other aspects of our church life. We have had two listening campaigns that involved the entire church. We have incorporated one-on-ones into membership programs and social action in general. One of the magical things about one-on-ones is their power to bring us together instead of all going in separate directions. We Unitarian Universalists are notoriously independent thinkers, and there is often a tendency for us to say, "That's not my main issue, so I'll let others handle it." But something about talking very personally about early influences and values that have motivated our actions has brought more willingness to support one another's issues. Maybe it is the recognition of shared values underlying our interest in different issues. Whatever the explanation, it works!

Dale was able to transform the way his church approached social justice work and build a vastly more powerful congregation by getting serious about the one-on-one. It's a compelling vision, but what are these conversations?

Simply put, a one-on-one is a thirty- to forty-five-minute intentional conversation with the goal of initiating a public relationship, learning each other's values, self-interests, and stories, and building power to move into action. One-on-ones are an open and exciting space to explore possibilities, challenge each other, and learn. What one-on-ones are not is a chance to chit-chat, pontificate about the issue or campaign you care most about, gossip, or exchange small talk and pleasantries. Maybe I thought the First Lady's hat on Sunday was ridiculous, but our one-on-one is *not* the time to go there!

So let's break all this down.

A thirty- to forty-five-minute conversation. Seems pretty straightforward, but let's be clear what that means. We sit down, with one other person, face to face. We put the phones away. We don't pull out a bunch of handouts, articles, or surveys. We spend this time truly focused on getting to know the other person, understanding their concerns and motivations, and figuring out how we might be able to work together.

An intentional conversation. One-on-ones feel different than most of our casual talking. We are trying to get somewhere together—a deeper understanding of who you are and how God is moving in our church or community to work for justice. We are trying to learn the key parts of a person's story and assess if they may be a potential leader in your efforts. A good one-on-one will cause both parties to reflect on their lives and assess new ways to advance God's kingdom.

Build a public relationship. Since power comes only through organized money and organized people, we build power through bringing people together. And building relationships is the only way to do that in a reciprocal way. The one-on-one is that key building block.

Remember, even though we are building public, and not private, relationships, this is a distinction in the type of relationship, not the depth. In one-on-ones we ask people who they are, where they come from, what excites them, and what makes them angry. We probe deeply to really understand the pivotal moments or experiences in their lives and how those moments or experiences have shaped who they are today. We learn about their dreams for themselves, their families, and their church. And we find common ground to move into action together. These are deep relationships, but they are public, focused on being accountable to each other to co-create our shared vision for our church and our world.

How Do One-on-Ones Work?

At almost every training session for one-on-ones, people ask for a script or a list of questions to ask. Sorry, but there is none. Since we are building intentional public relationships, we have to be in real conversation, fully engaged with the other person, authentically listening and responding to what they say. But that doesn't mean there aren't some guideposts or overall structure. For me, a useful metaphor is that one-on-ones are jazz performances, not classical. In a jazz performance, there is an opening tune and a set of predetermined chord changes that provide structure for the performance, but the notes that are created are still invented by the performer in the moment. So, here are the four basic guideposts, or overall structure, of a one-on-one conversation.

First, we clearly set up our one-on-one. That means no sidling up to someone during coffee hour and asking, "So, what have the most transformative moments of your life been?" We pick up the phone or approach someone directly and ask if we can set aside thirty to forty-five minutes to meet, and we explain the basics of the meeting. We might also include a "credential," a way of explaining who we are and contextualizing why they should talk to us. Or it might be citing a person who has suggested that you connect. For example, at my church we fairly regularly do one-on-ones, so I might call someone and say, "Hi, this is Alex and I'm a member of St. Agatha Faith in Action team. We are meeting with members in our congregations to learn about one another, build relationships, and figure out how we can act together to change things in our community. In my meeting last week with Ms. Lewis, she told me that she knew you had a lot of passion and knowledge about our neighborhood. Could we meet for about half an hour in the next couple of weeks?"

That's not so scary, right?

Now some people may not be willing to meet with you, but, when you clearly explain who you are, how you are connected, and what the overall purpose of your meeting is, as well as let people know that you are only asking for thirty to forty-five minutes of their time, you'll be surprised how often people will agree.

Congratulations! You've just set up your first one-on-one.

At the start of our meeting, we explain what you are doing and why one more time. Most people do not regularly do one-on-ones or even know what they are, so lay out the goal again, set the context of why you or your church are doing relational meetings, and remind the person of your credentials. This will take only a minute or two, but being clear here will spare you the embarrassment I had in the one-on-one (or date?) I described in the previous chapter.

And then, ask a question. This moves us into the second stage of the conversation, learning a person's story.

This is the real heart of the one-on-one, so these questions are vital. Since our goals are to build a relationship, understand a person's values and self-interest, and learn their story, we don't want to ask a factual question ("How long have you been a member of the church?") or an opinion or debating question ("So, what do you think of our president?"). We want to ask a person about themselves.

If I'm doing a one-on-one with a member of my church or another church that I'm organizing, I might ask, "What brought you to this church or the ministry you are a part of?" Or I might ask someone, "What things do you see happening in your community that you would like to change?"

And then you have to listen. Really listen. Open your mind and heart to really hear what they are saying. Don't move on to another scripted question; dig deeper. Ask what about the thing they talked about makes them angry, or ask why that is so important to them. Find out where in their own life that experience comes from. And keep really listening.

Over the course of the next fifteen to twenty minutes, we want to learn:

- Who this person is.
- What the pivotal experiences in their life have been and what those experiences have meant to them.
- What their dreams are, their vision for themselves and their family, their vision for your church?
- What keeps them up at night.
- What gets them out of bed in the morning.
- What issues they are concerned about enough to take some action.
- Who the key relationships in their life are.

Many of us assume that people will *never* share that kind of information with someone they barely know, especially in a first meeting; but, when you start having these conversations, you'll find that most people, even very introverted ones, love the experience of being truly listened to. When we challenge ourselves to fully invest in another creature made in God's image and likeness, and to find out about them, it's amazing how often they will be willing to share.

During this time, the person you are talking to might get curious in return and ask you about yourself. If so, great! This isn't a robotic interview; it's a chance to build a relationship. So we need to be willing to share ourselves in the same way. The ask may not always be clear; in fact, it might sound a little rude, but we have to hear the question behind the question, which is usually, "Who are you, and why should I want to be in relationship with you or share who I am with you?"

Many years ago, I was working on a campaign around children of incarcerated parents. One of my leaders told me she met a woman, named Edna, who was raising her six grandchildren because her son was in prison. I called her up and we set a time to meet at a coffee shop near her house. When she walked in, she took one look at me and said, "Well, shit! You are young and white! Why should I talk to you?" I could have responded with a heady, impersonal, and theoretical answer, "It's not really about me, it's about you and your story"; or I could have gotten offended, but, fortunately, I was able to hear the real question behind her inquiry. She was, a little bluntly, asking me, "Who are you? Why are you involved in this fight? And why should I trust that you are really committed to it?"

So I told her about growing up in Harlem and watching my friends get harassed by the police. I told her about families in my own church who were dealing with an incarcerated family member. And I told her how angry it made me to watch people I cared about get screwed over by our system and how that anger led me to becoming an organizer. I'm happy to say that Ms. Edna heard me, and we began a great relationship. She became a leader in the campaign, and a year or so later, her family became the first one in Illinois to do an extended family prison visit with more than two children, a key demand of our campaign that she had helped shape. In doing one-on-ones, we not only learn about others; we are forced to reflect on and clarify our own stories, values, and self-interests as well.

After twenty to twenty-five minutes of your one-on-one, you have probably learned a great deal about a person. If you have found a person who shares many of your values and may be a potential leader to join your work, you have reached the third stage of the conversation, sharing a vision. Now we shift slightly from learning a person's story and passion to sharing a little bit of the work we are doing and how we can address the issues that have come up by coming together as a powerful congregation.

Often we might start with a question, something like: "I really resonate with what you're saying. I get mad about that issue too. That's why our church is doing this kind of conversation. Have you ever thought about how we could really make a difference if we could move our whole church to act together?"

In the case of Ms. Edna, I shared a little about the campaign, and asked her to reflect on how different the issues would be if thousands of families like hers, as well as faith allies and service providers, came together and demanded change. In Dale's case, he shared a vision of how his congregation could actually make a difference by intentionally acting together. In sharing our vision and connecting it to what we have heard in the earlier phases of our conversation, we can bring hope to people that, together, we can make a change.

Finally, we move into action together by making some small asks or propositions of the person we are meeting with. This is where the rubber hits the road in an exciting way during one-on-ones. We find out if we have really been listening and understood where a person is coming from, if we have shared our own vision clearly, and, most importantly, we also learn if they are someone who is really willing to act on their values, or if they are just a talker (we all have those folks in our congregations).

Again, since this isn't a scripted interview, there isn't one perfect ask. I will often have a few potential ideas in my head when going into a one-on-one, but I work hard not just to wait for a chance to bring one of them up but, instead, to really listen to the other person. Maybe one of my preconceived ideas will fit perfectly, or maybe a better idea will grow out of our conversation. But the proposition might include things like asking the person to connect me with a few other people whom they think it would be good to talk to, joining me for an upcoming action (and maybe bringing one or two people with them), or attending a training and exploring joining our organizing team. In public relationships we build trust by making commitments to each other and fulfilling them, so the turn is where we really start to understand the intentionality of these powerful conversations.

And then you are done. Close out the conversation; don't exceed the time you originally set, and leave while the energy is still high. While you should never take notes during a one-on-one, since this immediately takes you out of the conversation and turns it into an interview, right after you leave, take five minutes in your car or on the train to jot down the important points of your meeting. Otherwise, details slip away, especially when you do a number of meetings. A one-on-one is a beginning of a relationship, not an end; so it's good to leave feeling energized and looking forward to more work together.

Why Do One-on-Ones Work?

In one of his parables Jesus says, "The kingdom of heaven is like a mustard seed, which a man took and sowed in his field; and this is smaller than all other seeds, but when it is full grown, it is larger than the garden plants and becomes a tree, so that the birds of the air come and nest in its branches" (Matthew 13:31-32). This is the perfect way to describe the one-on-one: a tiny simple act that holds within it all the creative potential of massive public actions and campaigns. The people of Jesus's time expected the messiah to come down from heaven as a powerful military conqueror, descending from on high to bring freedom and justice in one fell swoop, but, with this parable, Jesus says something very different. In doing justice work, we have the same idea. We expect fiery sermons and large marches, but, in reality, those things are built on the foundation of quiet, one-on-one conversations. God's kingdom will not be inaugurated as one mighty blast from above but, rather, is already among us and at hand, being created through seemingly small, insignificant actions. We need to faithfully plant and water these small seeds of the kingdom.

So why do one-on-ones do this so effectively?

We are a people of stories. We human beings naturally understand ourselves and relate to others through stories. All human civilizations have told themselves stories to explain who they are and how the world works. For decades before the Gospels were written down, they were told as stories, and people flocked to join the Jesus movement, based on the stories that the apostles and other early evangelists told. Stories move us, and reflecting on our own stories and the stories of others tells us who we all are.

Several years ago, as I was organizing a new church, I met an older woman, Ms. Maezell, who was retiring and said she was interested in maybe joining the social justice ministry. As we met for our one-on-one, I delved more and more deeply into her story, asking why, after a long career, she wanted to do even more work. She finally shared a powerful story. She had been born and grown up on a sharecropping farm in rural Mississippi, working in the fields with her parents. Her mother had practically raised the daughters of the white family that owned the plantation, but, when the children grew to be teenagers, Maezell watched this girl, whose diapers her mother had changed, insult her mother and talk down to her and berate her. Even as a teenager, Maezell says, she knew she was never going to allow herself to live with that kind of injustice, so all alone, she left Mississippi, took the train to Chicago, and started a new life for herself.

Hearing this story told me more about Ms. Maezell's values, character, and courage than any intellectual discourse or book club ever could. And sharing that story helped her forge a bond between us, paving the way for years of action together.

They move us past issues and into action. As the Unitarian Church of Evanston knew, talking about social justice can become a way that we each rant about the issue that we are particularly concerned about, complain that no one else gets it, and continue to act with the same small group of "true believers." I know that some churches even have different ministries for each justice area. By contrast, one-on-ones move us toward powerful action in two important ways.

First, by listening to each other, reflecting on values, and sharing stories, we can move past each person's individual concerns and build a much stronger and more unified voice. Understanding what experiences have moved a person to action makes it easier to move out of our own narrow sphere and think about another perspective. Even more importantly, we are much more likely to say yes to actually taking action when we are asked personally by someone with whom we are in relationship.

This lesson came home to me in the presidential election of 2012. See, every year I tell myself that I should volunteer during the election. I get inundated by emails from candidates and advocacy groups asking me to help, but, somehow, I never get up and actually do it. Then, a co-worker of mine, who had been volunteering for the past several months, asked me to join her for the campaign's final push, and, low and behold, I spent the final weekend of the campaign phone banking into Iowa, Indiana, and Wisconsin! Nothing had changed about my values or desire. I had just gotten a personal ask. So instead of always complaining that no one wants to do anything, I learned to go build relationships and ask people directly.

Second, one-on-ones provide the space to move us deeper into more challenging action. While e-blasts, Facebook messages, and tweets may be able to get us to take small, easy actions like sending an email or donating five dollars to a cause, moving into prophetic and more costly action, such as nonviolent protest, civil disobedience, directly confronting a powerful person or giving up whole days of work to attend lobby days or major actions, can sometimes require a push. And these pushes can only be effectively delivered face to face by people who have relationships with each other.

You can do it right where you are with what you have! So often we think that, to be leaders, we have to have some special degree, position, or talent. Leaders are pastors, or prophets, paid organizers or highly trained policy experts. Not people like us. But Jesus didn't call the most learned, eloquent people. He called everyday folk. Not everyone can get up and give a great sermon or write a theological discourse. And very few of us have the time or money to invest in advanced credentials. But, just like Dale at the beginning of this chapter, almost all of us can simply start having intentional conversations, setting aside an hour or two a week, and slowly transform ourselves into powerful leaders of powerful churches.

And rather than setting some unattainable or amorphous definition or path to change, one-on-ones create a clear concrete way to move forward. We can hold ourselves and our teams accountable to a regular practice of one-on-ones as a clear way to build relationships and power.

They are fun! And that is true even for an introvert like me. Deeply engaging with other people, sharing our core stories, hopes, and dreams, and moving into action together to strengthen our churches and transform our communities are truly life-giving experiences. Rather than feeling constantly burned out, frustrated, or despondent at the state of the world, we can reconnect to hope and power through one-on-ones. In fact, whenever I feel myself getting burned out, bitter, or uninspired, I schedule some one-on-ones to remind myself that I am not alone. God created something special in all of us, and one-on-ones let us connect to that part of each other.

Some Tips and Hard Truths

While I love and advocate for one-on-ones as the most essential ingredient in doing the work of justice, I think we should also go into them with our eyes open so we won't be surprised or easily discouraged. So here we go.

They won't all be good. Simply put, you will not connect with everyone. Imagining otherwise would be impossible. Sometimes you will discover that the person you are talking to has values that are very opposed to yours, and there will not be a lot to say. More often, you may find that people are too busy, or perhaps too wrapped up in their own concerns or their own egos to be people that you want to work with. Some will simply refuse to make actual commitments to action. Some will not be interested in anything unless they get to be up front and in charge. But even these one-on-ones are gifts, because they mean you won't invite the wrong people into action or planning meetings, and you will have clarified in a short amount of time that this person is not the right person to move with.

Sometimes you will not do a good job of connecting with someone. I have done thousands of one-on-ones, and I still regularly have some that go nowhere or I leave feeling like I really wasn't present or wasn't able to really sync up with the other person. As you keep doing them, you will have good conversations as well, and they will more than balance out the bad.

They will feel awkward. At least at first. While having one-on-ones is an incredibly natural thing for humans to do, we, as a people, are out of practice. We aren't used to skipping small talk and diving directly into deep and meaningful matters. In polite conversation, we don't talk about deep pain and cherished dreams. We rarely say, "Hey! Wanna meet up for a one-on-one?" Asking people to meet may feel hard, and even scary (it certainly is for me). And getting into the flow of asking deep questions, learning a person's story, and making the turn and putting forward an ask may seem incredibly complex at first. Just like sitting in silence to pray or swinging a golf club for the first time may feel very odd. But stick with it. After doing a dozen or so, the one-on-one rhythm will start to come naturally.

There are no short cuts. Just like with getting in shape, learning an instrument, or building a prayer life, building power takes regular work. And sometimes it will feel like WORK. I don't always want to pray, and there are days where my prayer feels unproductive or forced. But I have learned that I need to keep at it, and sometimes God is working on me even when I can't feel it. In the same way, sometimes we won't want to schedule one-on-ones, or we will have a few unproductive ones in a row. But we need to keep at it. Whenever I see that a church's or organizer's ability to turn people out for actions or meetings drops, or whenever I notice a drop-off in my own work, the first question I ask is, how have your one-on-ones been going? More often than not, I can look back at my calendar and see that I haven't been regularly meeting with people.

Cultivate courage and curiosity. These are often called the two "C"s of doing good one-on-ones. We need to bring courage to our one-on-ones to make ourselves pick up the phone and set them, and then also to be willing to ask deep, sometimes hard questions, to invite people to really reflect on their lives. We need to bring courage to actually make an ask or challenge someone to stop sitting around and take action. And we need to bring courage to be willing to share ourselves as well and be open to the same kinds of challenge.

We need to cultivate curiosity to really want to know and understand other people. If we are just waiting to talk about ourselves, make our specific ask, or get our point across, we are unlikely to really build strong relationships (can't you always notice when someone isn't really listening to you?).

When I finish a one-on-one, I often ask myself, "Where did you bring courage and curiosity to this conversation?" Or sometimes, especially if the one-on-one didn't feel particularly good or productive, I have to ask, "Where did I fail to bring courage or curiosity?" That simple reflection can help me assess myself and improve my one-on-ones.

Go Try It!

In the end, the only way to learn one-on-ones is to do them. So go make a list of ten people, call them up, and schedule meetings. Or even better, do this with several members of your church or organization so you can have a person or a few people to be accountable to and reflect with. Some may be awkward; some may not go well, but I'm willing to bet that if you sow a few of these mustard seeds you will be thrilled at the harvest or relationships, energy, and power that you can begin to create.

Are you ready to plant the seeds of change in your church and your own life?

Are you ready to go have some one-on-ones?

CHAPTER 6

Fishers of Men and Women
Outreach Tools

So, how were your one-on-ones? Most of us, even the shy or introverted sorts, after doing a handful, begin to feel more comfortable. We start to understand the process and feel a little less awkward setting up and initiating these conversations. Maybe you have even had a few that felt really exciting—you made a connection, discovered new energy, or found a new ally; maybe a member of your church shares your passion in a way you never knew.

While one-on-ones are the most vital building block of congregational power, there are several other key tools and ideas beyond the one-on-one. Exploring these will help us understand how to truly grow our churches to their full potential.

House Meetings

To begin with, let's apologize for the confusing name, because house meetings do not actually have to be in a house. They can be in people's houses or a church basement, a park, a backyard, a local coffee shop, or a McDonald's—really anywhere that we can get five to twenty people together for some uninterrupted conversation.

Like a one-on-one, a house meeting is a structured, public, relational conversation, but, because these meetings involve many more people they are focused to a larger extent on building a sense of group cohesion and on getting information and understanding issues. We do house meetings either to make contact and identify potential issues and new leaders or to bring people together to build a sense of solidarity and begin to create an action plan regarding an issue we have already heard about earlier. We can hold a house meeting with members of our congregation, with community members, or with a combination of the two. In either case, the agenda for the meeting is similar (and there is an example of an agenda in the appendix).

First, welcome everyone and offer a basic explanation of what you are doing. Something as simple as, "Hi everyone, for those of you who don't know me, my name is Alex, and I'm a member here at St. Agatha. We are holding house meetings like these over the next two months in our church and community to get to know one another better, learn about our neighborhood, and identify some concrete things that we want to work together to change." Then have everyone go around and introduce themselves. Some churches and organizations might include a little bit of education or an icebreaker here. One of my personal favorites is a quick Bible study "quiz" or a game to demonstrate how God is focused on justice for the oppressed.

Then it's usually good to ask people to break into pairs or small groups for about ten minutes and give them some specific questions to respond to. If we are doing a general congregational or community house meeting, we might ask people the following:

- What do you love about our neighborhood or church?
- What do you struggle with here?
- What are one or two specific changes you would make if you could?
- Why are these things important to you?

If we are focusing on a specific issue, we would obviously have more focused questions. While they were building the FORCE Project, leaders held dozens of house meetings with people with criminal records and spoke about the struggles they faced trying to find jobs. They asked one another where they had applied for work, what they found the most difficult, and what opportunities they were most hungry for.

After people have spoken in their pairs and small groups, bring them back together for a group discussion. Ask everyone to share what they talked about. This is where the magic of these kind of open discussions can happen. Are there similar themes? Ask questions like, "Did anyone else talk about that?" or, "Has anyone else experienced that?" If so, we can ask to hear more about that story, and see if heads nod around the circle. Probe deeper. Ask, "What does that feel like for you?" or "What does it say that so many of us are experiencing the same thing?" Soon, people will start chiming in and sharing their own stories and insights. Two exciting things happen here. First, we start to get a sense of what the really important or pressing issues are for people in our community. In a general house meeting, we might learn big things, like the fact that people are deeply angry about the quality of our local schools or the violence in our neighborhoods, or small but important things about our congregational life. One church I worked with realized they needed to start a pancake breakfast because their members needed more unstructured social time to get to know one another. Or, if we are doing our house meeting about an issue, we can learn what people want changed and begin to make a plan of action. For example, what the leaders of the FORCE Project learned was that what a number of people with records wanted most was to be able to work with youth to address violence or to assist people with substance-abuse issues. These realizations led to campaigns that eventually passed laws in Illinois to remove absolute barriers to employment for people with nonviolent records in some of those industries.

Second, when people begin to hear stories of other people experiencing the same struggles as they are, a powerful realization can occur. Instead of blaming themselves, feeling shame and guilt, they can recognize that systemic factors and bigger actors have been in play. They go from saying, "I can't believe my family is living in such a dump. I can't even always keep the hot water on, what a failure I am," to saying, "So many of us can't make ends meet, no matter how hard we work. Why are we charged such high rent for such crummy housing in our neighborhood? We have to do something about this!" Sitting with people in the same situation creates a real sense of togetherness and a conviction that we desperately need to shake off the depression and sense of failure that can hold us back. That's why we hold house meetings!

Once we've gained these new realizations, the last step to a successful house meeting is to call people to action. After all, what's the point of learning about new initiatives or recognizing that we are all facing similar struggles if we aren't going to do anything about it? Having a couple preset ideas about next steps as well as allowing new ideas to evolve in the conversation is usually a good mix. We can ask everyone who attended to join a larger follow-up action at our congregation. Additionally, we can ask who would be willing to host their own house meeting, either around one of the new issues we identified or as a continuation of the conversation we are having. Asking for people to step up to do some preliminary research or have an initial conversation about one of the ideas that was surfaced during the meeting can be another great step. And not only do all of these actions help get your congregation or campaign moving, but they also engage new people in taking ownership and leadership as well.

So if you're trying to learn about issues in your church or neighborhood, or explore a specific topic that you already have a sense is affecting people, maybe it's time to invite them over to the rectory or to your house.

Neighborhood Canvasses

How many of the people who live within a three- or five-block radius of your church actually are members of your congregation? How many of those people know someone in your church? And how many of them does your church know? And what's happening in their lives?

As many of our congregations have grown and aged, especially in cities, we've seen churches become less a local parish and more a church people travel to attend. We say that we want to serve our communities, or "seek the good of the city where you are" (Jeremiah 29:7), but we may not even really know our local residents.

So what do we do?

We canvass! We get a team of volunteers together from our church and go out and talk to people in our neighborhood. If your church already has an evangelization ministry that goes door to door, all the better, because the biggest hurdle is getting people over the shyness, embarrassment, and fear of knocking on a stranger's door.

The basics of a canvass are pretty simple. Assemble a team of volunteers who will spend about three hours on each canvass. Pick a set of routes from the blocks around your church; generally think about areas where there are a lot of houses that are easily walkable, and where you can get to the doors (locked buildings or gated-off communities tend to be hard for canvassers to enter and can lead to a lot of walking for very few conversations), or places where lots of people congregate. Get everyone together for a short practice and role play; make sure you have everyone's phone number and that they have yours; pair people off for confidence and safety, and hit the streets. It's usually good to have something that you can leave with people (a basic introduction and maybe an invitation to an upcoming event or action) and to have a basic report form for you and your volunteers to fill out after each conversation—nothing deep, just the person's name, address, some contact information if they will share it, and the basic points of the conversation. (Some clip boards and pens will be valuable here as well.)

Generally, if you are going to do a canvass, it makes sense to plan several, maybe each Saturday for a month, for example, so your members and leaders have a chance to get comfortable and start having fun, and so you have a chance to cover all the blocks around your church and are able to go back and hit doors you might have missed.

Knocking on strangers' doors can be scary, but if you go in pairs and summon a little courage, you can do it.

Take a deep breath. Knock on the door. Smile.

"Hi, my name is Alex, and I'm a member of St. Agatha down the block. We're out talking to folks in our community today to get to know our neighbors and learn about how we can all work together to make our neighborhood even better. How long have you been in the neighborhood?"

And, hopefully, we are into the conversation. Now, when we are talking to people at their doorstep, we aren't likely to have full half-hour one-on-ones; but this isn't your normal political campaign door-knocking where we are delivering some canned message and moving on. People in our neighborhoods have had plenty of that, and our churches don't need to re-create it. Instead, we are hoping to engage in real substantive, human conversation (maybe ten or even twenty minutes) where we learn about what concerns them, share some of our own concerns, and see if they would be interested in joining us for some action together. So we ask the same sort of questions we would in a one-on-one:

- What have you seen going on in the neighborhood? What do you really like? What concerns you?
- What would you like to see happen?
- What do you think churches in our community should be doing to serve our neighbors?
- Are any of your other neighbors concerned about that? Should I talk to them too? Want to talk to them together or introduce me?

And when we hear someone share a real concern or idea (my kids aren't safe on the street; I wish we had a program to clean up these empty lots), we ask more about the issue from their perspective and then see if they would be willing to work with us on it. If they say yes, that's usually a good time to ask them for their contact information so you can follow up as well. If they talk about an issue or concern that your church is already working to address, feel free to share info with them (having a few pieces of information about church programs can be helpful here, but don't overwhelm people with paper).

Leave with the energy high, shake hands, and head to the next house, taking a quick pause to jot down a few key notes from the conversation.

Now some people won't be home, and some won't be in the mood to talk. Some will even be rude, but when we are trying to introduce our churches to new people, there's no way around this. In my experience, more people will be open to talking than we would think; and when they aren't, just share your frustration with your partner and move on. The goal is to go and find the good conversations, not fight with the cranky ones. If we keep on moving, we can have several good conversations over the course of an hour. And if you have five or ten members on doors for two or three hours, your church might get to know fifty new people and sets of concerns in one afternoon! Not too shabby.

"Do What You Can with What You Have Where You Are"

Those famous words are from Teddy Roosevelt. I'm not sure what he was referring to in that historical moment, but his aphorism applies to organizing our congregations today. A big part of our work and planning can be simply using or tweaking the opportunities our congregations already have through other ministries or congregational life activities to create moments of relationship building and learning. Most of our churches are already serving the residents of neighborhoods, meeting in small groups, and holding social activities. We can do a lot of organizing work by simply recognizing and utilizing these opportunities.

The Church in the Basement: Where Mercy Meets Justice

My dear friend Pastor Robert Biekman led Maple Park United Methodist Church into deeper relationship with its community and more powerful action for justice with a few small changes.

My evolution as an organizer has been organic. When serving on the west side of Dayton, Ohio, gathering diverse groups of people to hold elected officials accountable for addressing quality of life issues like education and community safety, seemed the right way, if not the only way, to create real change. Only later did I realize that I was "community organizing."

Fast forward to Chicago, Illinois, where I serve the people of Chicago as the appointed pastor of a fifty-four-year-old faith community located in Chicago's Greater Roseland community, referred to by some as the "Wild 100s" because of the gang violence that can characterize its neighborhoods. Maple Park was built as a neighborhood for middle-class blacks. The intervening years have seen a rise in lower-income residents, but a large number of original Maple Parkers have made a conscious decision to stay in the neighborhood. This often makes for an interesting clash of class!

Like other mainline denomination churches, Maple Park's enrollment began a steady decline since the late '90s. However, Maple Park has historically had a heart for the community. It is in this connection to community that we have remained relevant, vibrant, and continued to thrive. It seems like Maple Park United Methodist Church always had a feeding ministry, but a few years ago the ministry was "rebooted." Collaborative partners joined the church and the Park Café was reborn. This feeding ministry where all are invited to "dine with dignity" now serves between eight hundred to nine hundred meals each month.

In our reboot, as we sought to bring our outreach and organizing lens to our ministry, two subtle yet profound changes to the structure of the café were made. First, the long tables were replaced with round tables, and, second, an intentional connection between the communion table and the dinner was made. At these round tables we promoted conversation, discussed key issues, and built relationships. As issues of justice arise (e.g., police accountability), it has been the church in the sanctuary (Maple Park's worshiping congregation) and the church in the basement (Park Café patrons) who have lifted their collective voices to effect change. Park Café patrons have come seeking mercy but left doing justice.

Over the past several years this work of justice with Park Café patrons has included teach-ins, Bible studies, and community meetings. Park Café patrons have boarded buses and gone to downtown Chicago to participate in public actions and distribute flyers in the neighborhood. We've seen this give hope, imagination, agency, and perseverance to people who don't feel they are in control of their destiny. And some have even started attending service with us, as they see the church as something new.

Dr. King said, "Religion that professes to be concerned with the souls of people and is not concerned with the slums that damn them, the economic conditions that strangle them, and the social conditions that cripple them is a dry-as-dust religion." As church rolls dwindle, it is essential that churches become creative in how we engage not only our congregations but also our communities.

Does your church have a feeding ministry? A clothing drive? Maybe a tutoring program or partnership with a local charity or school? I'll bet that you can find a way to add a relational component to these ministries that lets you get to know people, learn about their struggles, and identify ways to move into action together.

Think about when and how the members of your church interact with each other. Do you have coffee and donuts after worship? Arrange some brief table discussions around just one question, or ten-minute guided relational conversations between members on a given Sunday.

Do you have small groups or teams? Do you have ministries that meet on a regular basis? Ask them to hold a house meeting as a part of their regularly scheduled conversation one month.

Some congregations have even included short, guided one-on-ones between members during the church service itself, often by extending the passing of the peace or the homily time.

And by and large, people enjoy these moments. They learn something new, feel a more direct connection to the work of the church, and start to see the ways that their experiences and those of their fellow church members and your community drive the justice work of your congregation. With a little focus, creativity, and conversation, you'll be amazed how much you can do without having to schedule one new event.

Like when Jesus called James and John, are you ready to go into your congregation and community to be fishers of men and women?

CHAPTER 7

I Have Called You by Name

Leadership Development

Have you ever heard of a church that didn't wish it had more active leaders within its congregation?

In all my years of organizing, this might be the issue I hear most often, especially from pastors and people in church leadership; there just aren't enough people willing to step up and lead the work that needs doing. It's what we call the 20/80 rule. Twenty percent of the people do 80 percent of the work. I'll bet your work for justice is very similar. I know that every organizer I've ever encountered spends a lot of time wishing we had more leaders, more engaged leaders, more capable leaders.

But What Do You Mean When You Say "Leader"?

That question stopped me in my tracks. To be honest, I can't even remember who asked it. But I'm sure that I was bloviating about community leaders and empowering people directly affected by injustice. We organizers do this a lot. "Our leaders say . . ." or "We have to listen to our leaders" or "The leaders need to decide." But, I realized in that moment that I didn't know what I really meant when I said that.

I think I stumbled through some unclear explanation. As I think back on it, I realized that I was simply calling whoever showed up to our organizational meetings our "leaders." But what, or who, were they leading? And what is the definition of a leader, anyway?

Picture a leader in your mind. In the context of faith-based justice work, our images often fall into two categories: the preacher giving an impassioned speech or sermon (Dr. King at the March on Washington comes most readily to mind for many) or a person directly affected by injustice giving their testimony at a rally or at a meeting with a person in power.

While there is nothing necessarily wrong with these images in and of themselves, they don't tell us much about what a leader really is. Are all great speakers also leaders? Do all leaders have to be great speakers? And if not, what separates the wheat from the chaff?

At this point, most of us start mumbling words like commitment and charisma and maybe position, but we haven't really settled on any solid definition. Instead, we've laid out a series of ineffable concepts that are hard to clarify or assess. Or we rattle off a long list of skills and competencies: a great speaker, meeting facilitator, strategic thinker, and writer, who is deeply committed to our work and always shows up on time. No wonder we don't have enough leaders! We either don't really know what a leader is, or require a skill set so wide that *no one* could possess it!

As I struggled with this, I finally was presented with a plain and simple definition: a leader is a person with followers that they can do something with. It almost seemed too simple and straightforward to be true. But, as I thought about it more and more, it made more and more sense. If there is no one with you, no one following you, or no one saying that you speak for them, how can you be a leader? You might still be brilliant, an engaging speaker, a great writer, or a person of profound and deep moral conviction, but, if you don't have people who follow you (and sorry, I don't mean on Twitter), then you really aren't leading anyone.

What is so helpful about this understanding of leadership is that it moves us away from falling back on understandings of leaders that push us toward middle- and upper-class educated people (definitions that focus on education and background) and from the superstar, ultracharismatic definitions of leadership. Leaders are not the most eloquent people, or the people with the most sophisticated analysis, or the loudest people in the room. Leaders are the people who are rooted within themselves, their faith, and their community, and, therefore, have relationships so people follow them. And leadership, therefore, is open to all different kinds of people. To be a leader, you simply must either have followers or be willing to build public relationships to create followers. You can do this without a high school diploma and without ever having to make a speech!

In fact, it's pretty obvious that God does not look for the most educated, well-spoken, stereotypical "leader types" to build the kingdom. Moses was a famously bad speaker, going so far as to tell God, "Please, Lord, I have never been eloquent, neither recently, nor in time past, nor since You have spoken to Your servant; for I am slow of speech and slow of tongue" (Exodus 4:10). David is so unimpressive that his father does not even think to present him to Samuel when Samuel is looking for the next king. In fact, when David's father presents the son who seems the most likely choice, God has to tell Samuel, "Do not consider his appearance or his height, for I have rejected him. The Lord does not look at the things people look at. People look at the outward appearance, but the Lord looks at the heart" (1 Samuel 16:7). The apostles chosen by Jesus are notably not drawn from the leaders of the people. Even Jesus is born in a backwater town, as a member of a conquered people, to a poor father and mother. "Can anything good come from Nazareth?," Nathaniel asks when he first hears about Jesus (John 1:46).

How Do We Identify Leaders?

But, since we aren't Samuel and God won't just tell us who to anoint, how do we find leaders? I'll give you a hint: it's not by asking for volunteers from the altar! According to the old adage, insanity is doing the same things over and over again and expecting different results. Well, if that's true, we in the church are absolutely nuts! Because over and over again, when we want to start something new or bring in volunteers, we go up to the lectern at announcement time, explain why something is important, and ask people who are interested to sign up in back. When we do this, I've learned to beware of two types of people who show up over and over again masquerading as leaders. First, there are the people who just don't have enough to do. While it is nice that people have time on their hands, my sense is that there is usually a reason! They probably don't have a following of their own and aren't going to bring much besides another warm body to the table. Now this may be fine when we are trying to fill a bus to attend a public action or get folks to help cook hot dogs for the church social, but it's not very useful when we need people to actually lead something. Second, we usually find the set of people who have an axe to grind and are waiting to have some space to talk about it. Now they may be passionate about the issue you are working on, or they may be trying to make noise and be recognized, but they usually move alone and, boy oh boy, can they bring a group down!

So if altar calls aren't the answer, what is? Once again, we need to talk to people. And when I talk to people within a church, there are two sets of people I look for: the current indigenous leaders of the congregation and the people who want to be or could become leaders—the potential leaders.

The indigenous leaders within a congregation are those people we need to buy into a new program. They are the people who are respected by the community. They sometimes hold positions and titles, but that isn't always the case. You can usually figure out who they are by asking questions. Ask a few people things like, "Whom in your church do people really respect?" "With whom would you want to work on an important event?" "To whom would you listen if they asked you to take some sort of action?" "To whom do you go for advice or guidance?" "Who really gets stuff done around the church?"

At my home church, when I arrived, we didn't have a lot of justice work going on, which was odd, because we had an incredibly devoted pastor who preached about the issues regularly and a congregation with a deep commitment to service. The social justice work was led mostly by a group of nuns. The nuns were wonderful, and people at the church loved them, but, as white religious sisters in a black community, they were, by definition, outsiders. When one of them would get up to talk about an issue or event, people would clap, but it was clear to me that this justice stuff was seen as "that thing Father and the sisters do." Who were the indigenous leaders who people recognized as "us"?

I started watching as we walked around greeting everyone at the sign of peace. I noticed that people congregated around Ms. Gloria Seabrook. Then I saw that, during Mass or at events, Ms. Seabrook would snap her fingers or give looks and people would get up and move additional chairs, or go get started on the food. Retired after a career of working at the Chicago Housing Authority, Ms. Gloria had a big smile and a loud, no-nonsense voice and demeanor. She had been a member of the church for decades, and her son and grandkids were all active members. When something needed to get done, she was the one people looked to—an indigenous leader.

Another person I noticed early on was Mama Versie. She always seemed to have something in her hands for someone else, and she "adopted" me very early on when I joined the church. Mama Versie is more quiet than Ms. Gloria. But I remember a

Bible study where we were talking about saints. Father said that a saint isn't some distant person in heaven; they are a person who, every day, lives for others.

"Who are some saints you know?" he asked. Four or five people in the group blurted out simultaneously, "Ms. Versie!" I hadn't heard Mama ever use the words "social justice" or "structural racism" in any of our conversations, but, clearly, this was an indigenous leader.

I knew that leadership from these women would be crucial to moving our justice work to the center of the congregation's life. I talked to Ms. Gloria about helping to lead our work. "Alex, I got too much to do. You all need to do that stuff!"

"Ms. Gloria, you know folks in this church don't care what I have to say," I responded. "If we want people to get involved, they really need to hear it from someone they listen to, and, from what I've seen, that's you." So Ms. Gloria got up to recruit people to attend a massive public meeting called Take Back Chicago. She didn't get all the details of the event right, but it didn't matter. When she sat down, the congregation was *going* to take their city back! And, on a Tuesday evening, we all piled onto buses to take action!

Now the thing about indigenous leaders like Ms. Gloria is that they are busy. They usually already have taken on a lot of responsibilities. They are on the parish council, the deacon's board, the hospitality committee, and women's club. They are readers, choir members, and ushers. You absolutely need their buy-in to begin to make social justice a central concern within your congregation. But, for them to be a part of the organizing team, you are going to need to do two more things. First, you will need to identify and develop some additional leaders to join the team with them. And second, and maybe even more important, you need to ask the most important question: "In order to step into leadership of our organizing for justice, what will you be stepping back from?"

Be honest, when asking someone to step into a new responsibility, any new responsibility, within your church, how often do you ask this question? I know, I almost *never* asked it when I was beginning to organize. And I know that very few of the hundreds of churches I've worked with over the years ask it either.

Even in my own life, I almost never get asked this question. But as I've gotten older, and as I am now married and have two small children, I've recognized how important a question this is. Between my full-time (or more-than-full-time) job, my responsibilities in my own church with our Faith in Action team, as well as serving as a lector and member of the men's group, trying to be a good and supportive husband, and everything that comes with being a parent, as well as trying to find a few precious minutes of quiet prayer time and for self-care (not to mention to write this book over the past months), the idea of taking on any additional responsibilities feels overwhelming. Yet I'm constantly feeling pulled to do more. If only we reflected on this question when someone asks us to take on a new project, or when we feel called to some new work.

Asking or being asked this question transforms the conversation. It tells us that the person who is asking us to commit to something new also cares about us as people. They are thinking not only about the work they want to get done but about our health and development as a person. Now we can make choices about what our priorities are.

I'm often reminded of the famous prayer written in memory of Archbishop Oscar Romero:

It helps now and then to step back and take a long view.
The Kingdom is not only beyond our efforts, it is beyond our vision.
We accomplish in our lifetime only a fraction of the magnificent enterprise that is God's work.

Nothing we do is complete, which is another way of saying that the kingdom is always beyond us.

No statement says all that could be said.
No prayer fully expressed our faith.
No confession brings perfection, no pastoral visit brings wholeness.
No program accomplishes the church's mission.
No set of goals and objectives includes everything.

This is what we are about. We plant seeds that one day will grow. We water seeds already planted knowing that they hold future promise. We lay foundations that will need further development. We provide yeast that produces effects far beyond our capabilities.

We cannot do everything, and there is a sense of liberation in realizing this. This enables us to do something, and do it very well.
It may be incomplete, but it is a beginning, a step along the way, an opportunity for the Lord's grace to enter and do the rest.
We may never see the end results, but that is the difference between the master builder and the worker.

We are workers, not master builders, ministers not messiahs. We are prophets of a future not our own.

I keep a copy of this prayer over my desk, and give it to every organizer I hire, but I realize now that I should have shared it with every leader as well. The lines that especially speak to me are the call "to do something and do it very well." When we pick up one piece of work, we must put something else down.

After a conversation like this, as she was planning to retire from her job, Mama Versie joined the Faith in Action team and became one of the leaders of our efforts to mobilize our congregation. Now, she was the person who would go to different church groups, signing folks up for trips to the state capitol in Springfield. And soon, our church was regularly bringing twenty-five or thirty people on a work day! More important, I heard the conversation change. Led by indigenous leaders, people in the church no longer saw social justice as "that thing the nuns do." In fact, I remember overhearing a member of our congregation who wasn't on the Faith in Action team talk about one of our annual Springfield trips. "You know, that's what we do at St. Agatha," she said. "We are a justice church."

Indigenous leaders show the church who we are and who we can be. When we do the relational work of identifying and really engaging with these leaders, we can transform our congregations. But, they are busy, and they care about developing their church as a whole. To avoid burning them out, we need to identify, recruit, and train new leaders for the roles these indigenous leaders are putting down, as well as add to our organizing team.

So, how do we find and support these potential leaders? I have found over the years and in studying the scriptures to look for a few key traits.

They are ready and willing to take action. So many of us like to talk and talk about what is wrong but can't ever seem to get off our rear ends and actually work on making change happen. Real leaders are ready to take action. This doesn't mean they fly off the handle or jump at anything shiny, but they are not ones to just talk—they want to get things done. I think this is why Jesus is so hard on potential disciples: "And another said, 'I will follow you, Lord, but first let me say farewell to my family at home.' Jesus said to him, 'No one who sets a hand to the plow and looks to what was left behind is fit for the kingdom of God'" (Luke 9:61-62). That is harsh! But, in these and similar scriptures, I think Jesus is saying that real leaders take decisive action on their values. Because we see them acting on their faith, we want to act with them and are willing to follow them into action.

They are accountable. In the Sermon on the Mount, Jesus says simply, "Let your 'yes' mean 'yes' and your 'no' mean 'no'" (Matthew 5:37). Don't swear oaths about lots of things, just say what you mean. Real leaders are the same. They are accountable. They make commitments and not excuses. And when they say they will be somewhere or do something, they take that seriously and follow through. Because we can count on them, we want to be in relationship with them and we follow them.

They are teachable. Leaders don't know everything. Maybe, even more importantly, they know that they don't know everything, and therefore are willing to be trained and taught. Peter, the leader among the apostles (and the first pope!), stands out in the scripture not because of how much he knows but because of how frequently he is wrong. If Jesus were looking for leaders who knew everything, clearly he wouldn't have picked Peter! What Peter shows us in his frequent wrongness is that, like all of us, leaders are still learning and are willing to listen. We all know how irritating a know-it-all can be. True leaders accept that other people know things that they don't, and don't think of themselves as smarter or more important than everyone else. We follow them not because they know everything but because they are willing to learn from others.

They have a strong ego. That's right! A strong ego is not the opposite of being teachable. In fact, we hear so much about Peter because he is willing, over and over again, to put himself out there, to take risks for what he thinks is right, and to try to act on his values. Sure, in Matthew 14, when he tries to walk on water he gets scared and sinks, but, before that, he has the courage to speak out to Jesus and to step out of the boat! I always want to know what a person stands for. Does anyone want to follow someone who is wishy-washy? Leaders have a strong sense of who they are and what they believe. Because we know who they are, we can have secure relationships with them and follow them.

They have joy. No one wants to follow a wet blanket! Real leaders, while they may be serious, have a real sense of joy about them. In describing the first Christian community, the scriptures say, "They ate their meals with exultation and sincerity of heart, praising God and enjoying favor with all the people" (Acts 2:46-47). Yes, Jesus has died, and, yes, the disciples face persecution both from Rome and from their own people; yet they are filled with joy. We can even see this in leaders not known as touchy-feely types. Che Guevara said, "At the risk of seeming ridiculous, let me say that the true revolutionary is guided by a great feeling of love." Ossie Davis, in eulogizing Malcom X, said, "They will say that he is of hate—a fanatic, a racist—who can only bring evil to the cause for which you struggle! And we will answer and say to them: Did you ever talk to Brother Malcolm? Did you ever touch him, or have him smile at you? Did you ever really listen to him? . . . For if you did you would know him." Over and over, we see that leaders have joy and love inside them. We see that joy and we relate to it, and, therefore, we can follow them.

Identifying and developing new leaders, encouraging them to speak for themselves and develop their own power, is, for me, at the core of good organizing. One amazing leader I have worked with is Teleza Rodgers. Teleza shares her story here:

A few years ago, leading an assembly of over two thousand people of faith, I asked each candidate for Cook County state's attorney, one of the most powerful positions in our system, to make specific commitments to change. They had to give a straightforward yes or no answer and leave knowing that WE had the power to hold them accountable. It was for me a chance to use my voice in a way I had never imagined.

Just a few years earlier, this would have been unimaginable to me. I had struggled with mental health challenges, lack of education and addiction when I was young, and, consequently, had eventually been locked up. Even though I had turned my life around, due to my felony conviction, I was banned for life from the right/privilege to work in many areas. I avoided politics and any involvement besides voting. To God be the glory for the many people I've met.

After joining a new church, my pastor learned my story and asked me if I would be willing to be a part of the Social Action Committee. This led me to a one-on-one with Alex. As I shared my story, he shared with me that the things I was facing weren't unique to me; they came from systemic decisions. And he challenged me to take action to change, not only my situation but that of so many others.

My awareness and involvement changed because my knowledge increased as I worked with Marlon Chamberlain, the organizer of the FORCE (Fighting to Overcome Records and Create Equality) Project. I learned that elected officials work for us and that when we hold them accountable, things change. Each action I saw made me want to do more, and Marlon pushed me to learn new skills to step into these new roles.

I'm thankful to be a leader now of an organization led by people with records, for people with records. Due to our work, we have been able to change laws and restore lives, and all because we invest in challenging and developing the leadership of people with records like me.

What Teleza says is true. She didn't fit the "normal" image of a leader in terms of advanced degrees or eloquent preaching. But she is one of the central leaders of the FORCE Project and a vital friend and ally to me. So how do we develop more Telezas?

Invest in Recruitment, Training, and Development

When was the last time you read one of the Synoptic Gospels straight through? A number of years ago, as I went through the Gospel of Mark, I was struck by something that I hadn't noticed when just reading sections or hearing the lectionary readings. While we think a lot about Jesus's sermons, miracles, and public actions, in fact, Jesus spends an inordinate amount of time calling individual people to join him and just talking to his small group of disciples. In these sessions, Jesus is giving his small group of key leaders special instructions, guiding them in understanding his message and ministry, and providing insight into how to understand the parables and lessons he shares with the crowds. In essence, Jesus is doing what organizers would call "train the trainers" sessions. There is not a single chapter in Mark, up to Jesus's arrest, where we don't see him issue some sort of private teaching or calling to his core group of disciples.

Can we say the same? Do we spend some time every day, or in every meeting, focusing on how we are training and developing our core leaders?

We spend time preparing our sermons and presentations, trying to sign volunteers up *en masse,* and planning actions or educational programs. It's not that the Gospels don't show us Jesus preaching, healing, and leading public demonstrations. It's just that he also is very intentional about recruiting and developing individual leaders, who eventually build up the Jesus movement into the church we know today. Our churches should bring a similar intentionality to our processes of identifying, recruiting, and training new leaders.

Several years ago, a church I worked with asked me to work with them to develop a special day-long training for the leadership of all their different ministries on how to create healthy and sustainable leadership development pathways within all their various ministries. We built a four-step process for their ministries: Proposition, Engagement, Training, and Step-Back, or PETS. (Alright, maybe the acronym is a little contrived, but we should think about how we are caring for our leaders.) When we have identified a potential new leader, we initiate the following process.

1. Proposition

If we want people to do something, we have to actually ask them. And in order to ask them, we need to actually know what we want them to do. Think about the last time you hired someone or applied for a job. The job application laid out the expectations, work hours, and main goals of the job. The offer included a start date, the person to whom you would be accountable, the benefits package, etc. And the job was not offered to the first person the hiring manager bumped into on the street; there was a considered process to identify the best candidate. Yet, for some reason, we don't use any of these best practices when we recruit new leaders. Even if we avoid the pitfalls of doing the general altar call and actually identify a person we want to ask, we usually say something like, "Hey! Would you think about joining our social justice committee? We meet next week?"

It isn't clear what we actually want people to do, why we are asking them, what the time commitment is, or why it matters. Nor have we said why we want this specific person to join, or how it is within their vision for themselves.

When we ask in this way, we tend to get wishy-washy responses. Or people will show up to a meeting or two and then drift away. So we need to make a clear ask. Does your church have job descriptions for its different ministries? I'll bet you don't! (Even my home church doesn't, at least not that I know of.) Without a clear set of expectations, it is basically impossible for anyone to make a real commitment.

So when we think about recruiting a new leader and making a proposition, we think about four questions that we to answer:

- Why is this work important to the world, our church, and our community? What is our vision?
- What are we specifically asking this person to do and commit to?
- Why are we asking them? Why is it within their vision for themselves?
- When do we want them to step into this role?

This is what an actual proposition to me might sound like:

"Alex, we really want our congregation to have a much more significant impact in the issues affecting our neighborhood. We know that there is a ton of injustice that we need to address. But we need new people in our congregation to step up. I want to ask if you will be a part of a three member team to do a series of one-on-ones with members of our congregation over the next two to three months, identify additional leaders for this work, and then present a vision of it to our church. I know you really care about the injustice you see in our community and that you have a lot of history in organizing, so I think you would bring a lot to this work, and it would allow you to connect that passion to your church. Would you be willing to be a part of this team, starting next month?"

2. Engagement

Now, it would be great if everyone immediately bought in, 100 percent, to what your vision was, but that isn't how the world actually works. New leaders bring new perspectives and ideas, and that's actually a good thing. So after we make a proposition, we need to engage with the potential new leader, just like the negotiation that occurs after an initial job offer. Now there are some things that are, or should be, nonnegotiable (you can't be a part of the organizing team if you won't do one-on-ones), but there are others that should be on the table (we meet on the first Tuesday of the month, because that is how we have always done it).

So we have to discuss these with a potential leader. If you just want someone to replicate exactly what you do, you are looking for a cloning machine, not a team member. Are there parts of the job description that can be adjusted? What do they need to do in order to make this a priority? What new ideas do they want to bring and how can those be incorporated into the work? And, maybe the biggest question, what do they need to succeed in the role you are asking them to play?

Which brings us to . . .

3. Training

No one knows everything. Period. End of paragraph.

When Moses encountered God in the burning bush and was called to take a leadership role, he tried to demur, saying he was not qualified. And for so many of us, feeling like we don't know enough or don't have the skills can hold us back. On the flip side, as congregations look for people to step into leadership roles, the fact (seemingly) that no one else knows how to do things can restrict our efforts or cause us to favor the more economically stable, educationally advanced, and usually white and male members of our churches and organizations as leaders.

But, if we remember Jesus's ministry, we can see that Jesus called his potential leaders and spent a ton of time *training and preparing* them to go out and build the kingdom. Nearly every job has some amount of on-the-job training, with most also having a longer-term talent-development pipeline. And yet, in the dozen or so years that I've been organizing with congregations, it amazes me how few have any training and development program for leaders in their social justice work (or any other ministry for that matter). How can we expect to develop leaders in our congregations if we don't provide them with the tools they need to grow?

There are two big categories of training we need to provide: formal trainings and individual coaching or mentoring. Formal training sessions, generally for groups, are a great way to provide skills and tools as well as to teach key frameworks and ideas. They also give the whole church or team a shared experience and understanding to work from. At the same time, organizers and leaders meet regularly with new leaders to provide ongoing coaching and reflection. We can use these times to check in on how new leaders are living into the new skills and knowledge they have learned in trainings, as well as to share institutional knowledge. We also use it to build strategy together about where the person wants to go, and, sometimes, to push a leader to be their best self.

Is that a lot of work? Yes and no. Developing trainings and coaching new leaders certainly sounds like a lot. But so is continuing to do everything yourself, while bemoaning the fact that no one else will do anything. If Jesus can spend time in every chapter of the Gospel providing small group and individual leadership development, then surely we can do the same.

The other good news is that, unlike continuing to do all the work yourself, developing new leaders means we can let some things go. As long as we are willing to . . .

4. Step Back

For folks hoping to develop new leaders, this, sometimes, is the hardest step. After we have made a clear proposition, engaged with the concerns of the new leader, and provided appropriate training and coaching, we need to be willing to step back.

Sometimes this can take the form of you sharing space within your current work. Instead of you being the chair of your team, you now have a co-chair. But that means sometimes you won't get your way anymore. Or sometimes we are developing someone to take our place to allow us to take on a new leadership role or create some needed space in our lives. Either way, if we have asked people to lead and trained them to do so, we have to then allow them to do it. This may mean things don't go exactly as we wish. Maybe we feel we could have done a better job. There are certainly times in coaching that we may need to correct folks, especially if they are making a mistake you have seen or made before. But, on the other hand, we can understand that there are a lot of ways that God can work, and calling new leaders means respecting and supporting additional visions besides our own.

What Are We Inviting People Into?

Ultimately, leadership development is a process, and, therefore, we need to do it within a structure. After all, you don't start an exercise or new degree program without a plan for where you are going. Churches and organizations that do this successfully have a clear ladder or path for leadership development with three crucial elements that are shared with, and understood by, everyone.

First, the actual roles, and the skills and knowledge required for each, are written out and agreed to. Everyone knows what the expectations are of being on the social justice committee, or finance committee, or deacon's board. Second, there are regularly scheduled training opportunities. Often, churches join organizing groups, in part, for assistance and to share training resources with other churches. It's just easier if we know that we are going to do quarterly trainings for developing leaders. And finally, how and who we are engaging and developing as new leaders are woven into the fabric of our justice work and our other ministries. Part of being a leader means identifying and developing new leaders with you. And it also means rotating leadership roles and creating space for new leaders to grow.

So, whom are you developing?

Does your church have a process and structure in place to identify, recruit, and train new leaders from within your congregation and community?

What do you need to put down in order for your congregation to focus on building up new leaders?

CHAPTER 8

The Salt of the Earth

Agitation

Ask yourself a simple, but not comfortable, question: how often do you fail to fully live out your values?

For me, it is an awful lot of the time. I know that there is injustice in the world and I should take action, but it is so much easier to think "someone else will do it." I care a lot about my church taking an active role in the issues that are affecting our neighborhood, but I make excuses about why I am not the person to move the work forward ("I have so much else going on." "Shouldn't a younger/older/more directly affected person take the lead?"). I believe that, as a white person, I should be engaging with other white people and challenging them on their racist attitudes instead of forcing people of color to take on that burden as well, but it's so much easier to not rock the boat and face the possibility of upsetting someone or losing a relationship. I believe that we all need to vote, but I say to myself that nothing I do will *really* make a difference, so I stay home rather than joining the voter registration canvass. All of these are examples of how I am in dissonance; my actions are out of alignment with my faith and values.

Fear of failure. Cynicism. Laziness. Self-doubt. Concerns about rocking the boat, or not being taken seriously. Hopelessness. Fear of reprisals from powerful people. All of these things are like dirt that sits on our values, obscuring them from view, keeping us in dissonance, and holding us back from being the people God calls us to be. When we need to shake the dust off of our values, and move to act, what we need is agitation.

What is agitation? In an old-style washing machine, the piece in the middle was called the agitator. It shook up all the clothes, water, and soap, ensuring that everything got clean. To get our values clean we need a similar element. Agitation is an act of love in which we challenge a person with whom we are in relationship to take action to change their behavior and resolve their personal dissonance.

A few chapters ago, I shared an example of one of the most powerful agitations that I have ever received, when my mentor, Dr. Morris, agitated me around my behavior and attitudes, challenging me to check my ego and grow into a better organizer as a white man working with black churches. This was an extremely tough conversation for me, as well as for him, but I'm unendingly grateful to him for it, since it helped me grow into the person I am today (still imperfect, but closer to who God is calling me to be).

During the Sermon on the Mount, after proclaiming the Beatitudes, Jesus tells his audience that they are the salt of the earth (Matthew 5:13). Salt was a vital preservative in Jesus's time, helping to store and keep food fresh to ensure that people would have enough to eat. It was also a key source of flavor for food. So we need that salt. But salt also stings. It isn't always sweet or easy. If we are going to truly live the Beatitudes and serve as peacemakers, as blessings to the poor, and justice seekers, I think Jesus is telling us, we need (and we need to bring to others) a little salt, something to help freshen our faith and keep pushing us to act. We need agitation and to be agitators.

What Agitation Isn't

Before we go on further, let's clarify what agitation is not, since these concepts often get confused.

First, agitation is not irritation. While it certainly can get under our skin, agitation is not simply meant to offend people, put people down, or puff our chests up about how morally superior we are. While sometimes the line between challenging someone and making them feel beat down can be a fine one, we always need to pay attention to it. I remember a number of years ago, I was the organizer for our campaign around children of incarcerated parents. Our leadership team for the campaign was made up of families with incarcerated people, pastors, community activists, and lay leaders from congregations across the area. The team of fifteen or so people met every month planning strategy. I believed then, and still do now, that teams need to be accountable to one another, and be willing to challenge one another. One way we can do this is by being on time. But I'm not proud of what happened next. One of our key members had asked to have our meeting moved, since she had to drive over an hour to each meeting. We had agreed, but she was still late. I announced to the team that they needed to "really hold her accountable" for being late. No one was willing to do so, so I announced that they needed to get serious about really winning this campaign. When the leader arrived, I came down on her hard. "You claim that you really care about helping children, and you want to be a part of this team," I said, interrupting the flow of the meeting. "You asked us to move this meeting further north for you, but you still walked in late. I think you should apologize to everyone here and make a real commitment to respect all of our time."

Now because we had had a very positive relationship in the past and because she was used to my fairly abrasive personality, she actually took it well. But later, one of the pastors in our group approached me, very upset about the whole interaction. I think I brushed him aside at the time, but, looking back, I realize that he was right; I wasn't focused on helping my leader grow at that moment. I was simply trying to show what a badass organizer I was. And that attitude came through.

Second, agitation isn't just confrontation. When people are doing wrong, Jesus is very clear that we should challenge them. This is especially true of our public officials. Like Moses before Pharaoh, Jonah in Nineveh, Jesus confronting the scribes, or our modern-day prophets like Martin Luther King, Dorothy Day, and Oscar Romero, we are certainly called to decry the abuse of the vulnerable and call for people to enact gospel justice. But, in a broad sense, confrontation is about pushing people to change their behavior to conform to *our* values.

Agitation, on the other hand, is focused, very specifically on the other person—their values, their vision for themselves, their potential, and their concerns about their lives, family, and community. That's why agitation must be an act of love. You have to love someone to be willing to take the risk of offending them, being seen as mean, or even of losing the relationship, to agitate them to grow.

This means that, first and foremost, to agitate a person we must be in relationship with them. And the deeper the relationship, the deeper the agitation. Think about it. Can't you hear things from your closest friends that you would never be able to accept coming out of the mouths of strangers or mere acquaintances, especially if they are speaking hard truths? When we are in relationship, the person we are speaking to knows and trusts that what we are saying is coming from a place of deep and genuine respect and concern. The reason I could hear Dr. Morris's deep challenge to me was that I knew, from our long-standing work together, that he cared about me. When we have just begun to get to know each other, you can agitate me around smaller things (my willingness to listen or my ideas about a campaign), but when we know each other deeply, I can hear you when you go very deep into my core values.

A strong relationship sets the foundation for the second thing we need in order to do meaningful agitation: a clear understanding of the person's values, concerns, and vision for themselves. During our one-on-ones, we get to know each other so we can learn what really makes a person tick, what is most in their heart, and where they feel God is calling them. Dr. Morris knew that, at my core, I deeply cared about racial justice and about being an organizer who truly developed leaders.

Once we understand a person's values, there are three crucial questions we must answer for ourselves and then ask them to recognize for themselves. First, we identify a point of key dissonance. How are they acting in a way that is contrary to their values? Second, we envision the person's public life if they were fully living out those values. What do we hope for each other? What is our vision of the greatness God is calling them to? Third, we try to understand why they are in dissonance. What attitude, behavior, or belief is blocking them from living into the person they are called to be. And lastly, we issue a challenge for the person to make a choice, take responsibility for their dissonance, and act to resolve it.

In my case, Dr. Morris recognized that my deep value was in dissonance with my disrespectful behavior toward leaders. He envisioned that I could indeed be a GWM (Good White Man) and an organizer who truly built power and brought about change; and he wanted to see me live into that vision. But he also saw that my ego was getting in the way of God's vision for me. And so he challenged me to step back, check my own ego, and focus on truly building people up. Recently, my friend Rachel Lyons faced a similar situation in the church where she worked. *Three years. After three years of work at a church in downtown*

Chicago as an organizer and social justice coordinator, my work was finally getting recognized and my ministry was building some momentum. I was getting asked to facilitate staff meetings, and then was invited to leadership and parish council meetings to represent all of the social outreach ministries at the church. After a few such meetings, Daniel, a long time, well-loved, high-level staff member (and arguably the person who held the most power and influence on staff), asked me to meet with him. We were talking about an upcoming organizing event with other churches and elected

officials. At one point during our conversation, Daniel made a comment that was racist and classist and that greatly undermined what I saw as the mission of the church and my personal work. I froze. I did not push back or name what had occurred. We finished the meeting, and I walked away.

But, after a few days, I couldn't shake the conversation. I sought out my colleague who ran our youth ministry programs and not only taught social justice principles in her programming but also lived out those principles in her personal life. I knew I could trust her. I went to her office and shared what had happened in my conversation with Daniel, and I also shared my inaction. She listened and empathized, noting she too had struggled in conversations with him. We both knew these were not isolated situations. She asked how I felt during the conversation with Daniel, and I shared my fear of speaking up to challenge him, the tightness in my chest, the way I doubted how my response would come out and if it would even have an impact. After a moment of quiet, she looked at me and said, "The thing is, we both know this will just keep happening until someone says something to him."

I nodded and looked away, then looked back at her, feeling frustrated that she was saying what I already knew instead of giving me a solution. "Yep," I said, "that's how this works. People see what they can get away with, what they can say out loud, and then they just keep getting away with it. And then nothing changes."

"Exactly," she said, "nothing changes. You've worked really hard to build a ministry here, from a position that didn't exist a couple of years ago. Right? And now you have access to spaces and conversations with Daniel that some of us don't. Think about it: what would it be like to have our justice ministry grow and have a staff that actually embodies and practices what you and your leaders are preaching and teaching?"

I thought for a second, still a bit discouraged, and said, "Well, that would be amazing, if it could ever happen. I don't even know what that would take, to get everyone there, to get Daniel there. I . . . I just totally lost my words with him, you know? I wasn't prepared."

My colleague waited a beat, then simply asked, "When is the next parish council meeting?"

"A week from Friday," I replied. She didn't say anything back right away, and I took the silence as a nudge to get prepared. Of course, I realized I now had time to find my words, to be ready, to build up my confidence. I had time to prepare to take a risk. I had some work to do, so I said thank you, smiled at her, and left her office.

This agitation was steeped in a relationship of trust, respect, and accountability. Because my colleague knew I was sitting in dissonance, she was able to remind me of all I had put into this ministry and ground me in a vision that I had shared with her in many conversations—a vision that included church staff and members all embodying our values of justice, equity, and compassion. She didn't let my frustration, doubt, and self-pity stop me from taking the action that would actually get me and our church closer to that vision, closer to our mission.

For the next meeting, I chose to imagine my leaders with me in the room. I wasn't just speaking up for myself; I was speaking up for all the folks who were counting on me to ensure that our collective shared values were upheld. When Daniel made an offensive comment, I hesitated, but eventually spoke up in front of everyone and named why I was uncomfortable with what he said. Daniel took my response better than I anticipated, listening and nodding as I spoke, saying a quick, "Thanks, good point," and moving on in the agenda. After the meeting ended, I found agreement and affirmation about what I said from several folks around the table. While this one instance didn't completely change Daniel or our staff culture, it did create more space for truth and shifted the power of one conversation. Daniel and I continued to work together in one-on-one and group meetings, and while our relationship certainly wasn't easy, we grew to be more honest and direct. And that shift gave me more fire and energy to face powerful people again and again when they were saying and doing harmful things.

I can't imagine this was an easy conversation for either Rachel or her co-worker, but we can see how important this agitation was. Her colleague knew her and knew that more than anything what Rachel needed was to be challenged to make a choice and to be the person she was called to be, a person who stands up when she sees racism and injustice.

What We Do Instead of Agitating

Challenging someone to deal with the ways they are not living up to their faith calling and values and to take responsibility for changing them is very uncomfortable for both parties. So very often, we try to get out of these conversations in a couple key ways.

First, we problem solve for the person. Imagine if, instead of challenging Rachel, her colleague had said, "Wow. That's really frustrating. Do you think you could find a way to avoid these staff meetings or this co-worker in the future?" or maybe, "How about if I take him aside and ask him not to speak that way in front of you anymore since it bothers you so much."

Seems pretty good, right? What a caring person!

But there is a real problem here. Remember, at her core, Rachel is the social justice coordinator of the church and feels called to create change, both internally and externally. To be that person, she needs to be able to challenge racism and classism wherever she sees it. Instead of respecting her as an adult, this kind of "help" would have been treating her as a child who needed her hands held. This kind of offer to help wouldn't have been based in concern for her but rather in fear or unwillingness to make her uncomfortable. In problem solving for Rachel, her co-worker wouldn't have helped her grow into her ministry at all!

The second thing we do instead of agitating is simply avoid the issue. It would have been really easy for Dr. Morris to simply not agitate me. He could have turned a blind eye to my behavior and simply let things continue as they had been. It's so easy during a one-on-one or when we are observing a person's actions, when we identify a point of dissonance, to simply change the subject. To spare my feelings, Dr. Morris could have simply ignored the problem, maybe talking to me about different campaign strategies, or started assigning me less time with older leaders of color. This certainly would have meant less emotional trouble, and less risk, for him. It would have been easier for me than actually dealing with my dissonance. But it certainly wouldn't have helped me grow. And it wouldn't have advanced our work in the direction it needed to go.

Finally, when we encounter dissonance, we often make excuses for people. We tell them it is okay that they aren't living out their values. I remember a conversation with one of the leaders of our FORCE Project, whom I'll call Charles. I was asking that he chair a meeting with an elected official about a bill to seal felony records. Charles didn't have a high level of education and felt intimidated by the official, and even by the other pastors and church leaders on our team, many of whom had advanced degrees and high levels of professional achievement. So he was trying to back out of it.

"Can't I just share my story, like I've done before?" Charles asked. "I don't have the time to prepare for the meeting, and it would be better to have someone be the chair who can really speak the same policy language."

I took a deep breath (yes, despite my "tough guy organizer" persona, when I'm about to do an agitation, I still get nervous), and said, "I remember you helping to found FORCE because you wanted people with records, people like you, to be driving the conversation about issues affecting you," I said. "Did you mean that?"

"Yeah, man, you know I do! I'm out here fighting for this bill!" he answered.

"Okay, but what happens if, every time people with records are being discussed, you give up your voice and ask someone else to lead the conversation?" I replied.

He stared at me for a second. It was a tough moment. I was worried, and, deep inside, there was a voice telling me, "He has kids at home. He works long hours. He doesn't have a ton of experience in legislative meetings, and this kind of space can be intimidating. Let him do what he is comfortable with."

And I almost backpedaled and said all that. But before I could lose my nerve, he spoke.

"You're right," he said. "If I don't speak up for myself, who's gonna do it for me? When is the prep meeting?"

After the meeting, during which the elected official agreed to co-sponsor our legislation, we were doing evaluation and the leader leading the evaluation asked Charles what he had learned.

"I learned that I need to have courage," he said. "I learned that I can step up and take the lead, and that I need to not let other people speak for me."

Charles led a number of legislative meetings around this bill, and others, which eventually became law, and developed into the leader he wanted to be, a person who led the conversations about his own rights. But it still scares me to think how I could have let him down by making excuses for him.

Three Agitations Every Church Needs

There are many times and opportunities for agitation in our lives and in the work of our churches to become powerful. We all experience different dissonances, and the tenor of our relationships is different. However, I have found that there are three big dissonances that I and other church leaders need to do agitations around with great frequency.

Agitating for Leadership

Most people are hesitant to make commitments, especially to take on a leadership role, which is why we find that our churches so regularly fall victim to the 20/80 rule. It's not that we don't care about the project or issue, but fear of failure, our busy lives, self-doubt or laziness get in the way. We just aren't quite ready or willing to commit. When this happens, we need agitation. We need someone to tell us, "I know how much you care about this project and the effect it could have on your life, our church, or our community. You have told me how much this matters to you. But if you aren't willing to commit to making it happen, no one will do it for you. So are you willing to step up and lead, or will you let this thing that matters to you fall down?"

Agitating for Accountability

Churches and volunteer-led groups suffer more than most from a lack of follow through. People make commitments at a meeting but a few weeks later, nothing has happened. Whether it's showing up on time (or at all) to meetings or events, making the phone calls or doing the one-on-ones we've said we would do, or creating a set of materials, people not following through can kill the morale of a team and bring your campaign to a halt. We generally either just let the action go, do it ourselves, or write the person off. But, instead, to build a strong core of leaders, what we need is agitation. I have never wanted to be a person that can't be counted on, and I'm sure that you haven't either. But, sometimes the business of life, or apathy, or hopelessness just crushes that value. At that time, we need someone to sit us down and say, "I believe that you can be a powerful and important leader. But, when you don't fulfill your commitments, it hurts the work of our team, and it makes other people believe that they can't count on you. Do you want to be the person that no one counts on, or are you ready to make a commitment to making your yes mean yes and your no mean no from now on?"

Agitating for the Courage to Confront

Lastly, doing justice means being willing to move into public action and confront people in power. But confrontation is not always easy for good church folks who have been (falsely) taught that following Jesus means being nice. So, over and over, as we begin to take on justice issues, we must confront the dissonance people face in wanting to stand up for gospel justice but not wanting to offend. Again, in this space of dissonance, we need agitation. We need to be reminded of the Jesus who overturned tables. And we also need to be reminded of the real cost to real people's lives if we don't win the issue we are working on. We need to be asked, "People are hurting, or even dying because of the issue that we are working on. Do you really think Jesus would be willing to stay quiet in the face of this kind of oppression? And is it more important to you to stay on good terms with decision makers and allow everyone in our congregation to stay in their comfort zone than it is to follow Jesus's example and publicly challenge injustice?"

Is it Worth It?

Man! This agitation stuff sounds tricky. And hard. And scary. Do we really need to do it?

Yes! Because our other choice is to avoid dissonance, or make excuses, or overempathize and try to solve their problems for them. And if we do that, we cannot simultaneously complain about how we don't have enough leaders. Nor can we really claim to care about the people we are in public relationship with or value their development. We are choosing our own comfort with the status quo over the needs of our communities and the best interests of our leaders. If I do not show up to a meeting about something important to me or do nothing while decisions are made that go against my core values, I feel terrible. When I know something is wrong, but I do nothing to stop it, I feel guilty when I see the effects of that thing come to pass. Or when a project I care about sputters because I was lazy and didn't step up and take a leadership role, I want to kick myself.

Agitation is an act of love because we need to love our leaders, team members, and partners enough to risk our own comfort to make sure they don't feel guilty and lazy. We need to challenge one another to grow into the people we are called to be, and the people that our churches, organizations, and communities need us to be.

In explaining agitation, Jim Fields, a mentor of mine and great organizer, draws a flower on the board or flip chart and asks people what that flower needs to grow into the biggest, healthiest, most beautiful flower it can be. A list develops. Sunlight, water, soil. Eventually someone says fertilizer.

"What's fertilizer," Jim asks. "What's it made up of?" The crowd, especially if it's church folk, gets a little uncomfortable.

"Manure," someone says eventually.

"And what's manure," Jim asks.

Finally, someone will say it: "It's shit."

And they are right! To grow to its fullest, a plant needs some shit! It's the way God designed our world. And we are the same way. To fully grow into the leaders we are called to be, we all need a little shit. That's what agitation is. The shit that nourishes. The salt of the earth, that stings but preserves and brings flavor.

Right now, I'll bet your team or church has leaders or potential leaders who are sitting in dissonance, not acting on their faith and values. They need someone to challenge them. And you and your church need them to step up and take action. Are you willing to love them enough to bring a little shit?

CHAPTER 9

Gathered Together

What Is a Powerful Church and Do We Want to Be One?

"Where two or three are gathered in my name there am I in their midst," Jesus tells us (Matthew 18:20). It is telling that Jesus calls us into community, to gather together. Our faith, he says, cannot only be about us individually, but how we move as believers. And the work of faith-based organizing cannot simply be about individually transforming the way we approach justice; we must use the tools from the previous chapters to transform our congregations as well.

So What Is a Powerful Church?

Since power is the ability to act, to create, control, or prevent change, at its core, a powerful church is a church that is able to drive change, a church that those in power know that they need to reckon with. Sometimes, as activist or justice-oriented churches, we will talk about issues, perhaps even preach about them, share announcements about opportunities for education or action. We might create some sort of public witness, like a peace flag or Black Lives Matter banner for their congregations. But are we really creating change? Can we get things done? Are we powerful?

Sometimes I think about it this way: does my local city council person know my church? Do they know that when we call from the church, we actually can speak on behalf of our membership? And do they, therefore, respond to our call and take action? What about our state representatives? Mayor? Congresspersons? Governor?

That's easy to think about if you are a massive congregation of thousands, but how can our little old, average size congregation become a force to be reckoned with? And what changes do we need to make to the way our congregations operate to allow this to happen?

These are the real questions we must tackle, and they are the same questions that people will be asking, whether they say the actual words or not, when we begin to have our one-on-one conversations. So, I asked my dear friend and colleague Christina Rice-Martin how she and her church made this shift. Here is what she said:

Organizing was a foreign word to Kingdom Baptist Church. Our church had been in the Austin community of Chicago's West Side for over forty years but realized that if we wanted to see changes in our community, we needed to be more prominent and effective, which is how our church was introduced to Alex and the Community Renewal Society.

At that time, our church had a growing young adults group, and the pastor decided that he wanted the young adults to be the instruments of the change that needed to take place. He felt this would be a way to keep us not only involved in church but get us engaged in the community. While the pastor and several older members were a part of our team, Kingdom was open to putting the young adults in the forefront.

Eight to ten of us came together for a one-day training, which was followed by a series of one-on-ones. That was where we found out who was ready for commitment and who wasn't. We initially began to canvass the neighborhood and survey to see what the people said they needed and wanted to see from their local churches. At first it was intimidating to go out. I love people, but I'm nervous talking to strangers. With my team around me, though, I took the leap. Then the church got involved in local meetings and met with our elected officials to discuss community issues. The more the church got involved, the more I got involved, gained new skills, and my position within the church and CRS grew.

That year, we traveled to the state capitol in Springfield, and we had so many members that we almost took over a whole bus! Only one other church could fit. While our pastor, deacons, and members all attended, once again, the young adults took the lead. We had a meeting set up with our senator, but she wanted to ignore us and at first refused to come to her office for the meeting. We decided to camp out in her office, and I told her secretary to let the senator know that our church delegation wasn't going anywhere until she came to speak to us! We meant what we said! Finally the senator came out, and we met with her. We got what we wanted. That feeling was amazing.

What started out as just volunteering my time to learn what the organization was about turned out to be something that has changed my life forever. In 2014 our church hosted the Martin Luther King Day Faith in Action Assembly, where over one thousand people came together to confront public officials and ask them to commit to the issues that we had come up with from our listening campaign. I was elected to lead the action along with a co-host. I was so nervous and scared. I always said that I hated public speaking. That day I faced my fear, which also boosted my confidence in so many ways. A girl who got nervous speaking to a crowd of two was now able to lead a crowd of over a thousand. All our work, meeting with public officials, and chairing meetings led me to be on the board of CRS and to growing leadership positions within my church.

Kingdom Baptist was a relatively small church, with no particularly historic stature or notoriety in their community; and yet, over the course of just a year or so, they became powerful— able to make things happen, and get reactions from significant policy makers. So let's look at the ways in which they changed how they moved as a church to have a greater impact on their community and world.

Build a Team

In the scripture from Matthew that started this chapter, Jesus says two or three have to be gathered together for him to be among us. Jesus knew that his radical mission that would become the church had to be done together. So the first thing Kingdom Baptist did was build a team of leaders.

Often after an initial one-on-one with a pastor, when there has been a strong connection, a sense of shared vision, and a desire to move forward, when we meet again to get to the next step, the pastor will say something like, ". . . and I've got the perfect person to head this up!" Early on in my career, I used to celebrate when I heard these words. "Alright!" I thought. "I know who my point of contact is going to be! I'll meet with them, and then on to the next church!" I would meet with this leader, and move quickly into plans for educational forums, or recruiting people to attend an action.

But over and over I found the same thing. After an initial honeymoon period of excitement, the person would start to feel burned out. Or they would be regular attendees to actions and strategy committees but could rarely bring more than a few people from their church. Or they would become disheartened by the fact that they couldn't seem to transform their congregation. And, after a while, I would hear them say, "Alex, I've just got too much on my plate. I still really believe in this work, but I need to step away." And the congregation would be back to square one.

It took me a while, and the guidance of some more seasoned organizers, to wrap my head around the fact that this work is too big for any person to do alone. A church needs to build a team of leaders to drive the organizing of their congregation. So before we get into issue campaigns, public actions, or meeting with elected officials, we need to focus on these core teams.

But the word "team" can be confusing. As regularly as we use it, we don't always really know what we mean when we say "build a team" or what the components or mission of a team is. So here is my working definition:

> *A leadership team is a group of people who take responsibility collectively and individually to engage the entire church in building power to advance God's kingdom of justice.*

I know that I've sat on plenty of committees where only a few people did all the work. When we make the move to become a powerful congregation, we have to make the commitment to take our responsibility as a member of a team seriously. We may only be called to give an hour or two a week to the work, but we need to really devote those few hours and accomplish the things we commit to. And, as a team, we must be willing to hold ourselves and our team members accountable to the work we are called to do.

Won't some people leave if we set these kind of standards? Yep! But we developed a saying in thinking about church and leadership development—"you choose who you lose." While St. Paul may be able to be all things to all people to bring them to

Christ, I know for sure that this is beyond us. So the way our teams and churches act will not work for everyone. We can act with no accountability, allowing anyone to "join" a committee or be called a "leader" without any real commitments or expectations; but the people who are actually interested in moving with intentionality and getting things done will leave or maybe never come. In fact, in Christina's story, she even said that by being accountable to holding one-on-ones, their team "found out who was ready for a commitment and who wasn't."

My rule of thumb? I'll take three people who are serious about moving into action and being accountable over ten who want to just show up to meetings. Because starting with those three, we can build and recruit. But if we set a team culture that lacks accountability, it doesn't matter how many people we recruit; either nothing will get done, or it will get done by only a few.

How big should your team be? Simply put, your team should be big enough to relationally engage your entire congregation. Teams that are made up of five to twenty-five members, or 5 to 10 percent of the active membership of the church seem to be about right. And since the goal of the team is to engage your entire congregation in powerful action, your team must also represent the different segments of the church. Do you have multiple services? Then folks from each service need to be on your team. Is everyone on your team over 65, even though your congregation is multigenerational? Then you have some work to do in terms of representativeness. Are there members from your church's different ministries on your team? At my home church, our Faith in Action team makes sure that we have people from the women's and men's groups, the choir, the Knights of Peter Claver, and the Ladies Auxiliary, the Golden Age Group, and both the 8:00 and 10:30 Masses. That way, we not only make it easier to ensure that our team is hearing from our whole church, but it also allows those members to build deeper relationships and become stronger leaders within their ministries. It also facilitates getting the whole church ready for action; we already know who will be signing members up from each ministry and Mass.

So the first practice of powerful congregations is to move away from having just the pastor or one leader drive all the work and to build an accountable and representative team. If you are that pastor or leader, don't worry about public action, educational forums, movie screenings, or anything else. Focus on finding and developing leaders to form the nucleus of an accountable team before taking on anything else.

This leads us to the second key practice of powerful congregations.

Focus on Developing People

Many churches that want to pursue social justice seem to have a different forum, teach-in, or letter writing campaign every week. These activist congregations are constantly talking about the issues. Most of the time it seems to me that there is a core set of true believers who do almost all the work and rarely expand their ranks.

Powerful churches, instead, spend a great deal of time and energy on developing people. As we discussed in the chapter on leadership, these congregations focus on identifying new people and helping them grow into suitable roles. Jesus focused a huge amount of his time on developing the leadership of his small group of key disciples. The letters of Paul, which make up the majority of the New Testament, are basically coaching for local churches and leaders. Kingdom Baptist began by assembling a specific set of leaders, asked each of them to be involved, provided in-depth skills training, and then developed a relational outreach plan with ongoing coaching, all before ever moving into action on an issue.

While most of us ask, "Who can we possibly get to do this job that needs to be done?," powerful churches ask the question, "Who is the right person to fill this role and what training and support can we provide to help them do it?" Or, even better, since we start from a place of relationship, "I've developed a relationship with a new person; what role can match their talents and passion with the needs and desires of our congregation and community? And how can we support them to grow into this role?" Imagine how different our churches would look if we switch these questions and approaches?

Kingdom Baptist used the tool of organizing and the social justice ministry to develop the skills and leadership of a set of emerging leaders. Their church leadership supported these leaders, and, as a result, the church became more powerful, won change in their community, and kept a key group within their congregation engaged and energized. They could have asked the same people who run everything to take over their new justice ministry as well, or just let the young adults go off on their own and then ignored them and this new "justice stuff." But instead, the church saw that developing a new core of young leaders was what the church needed and that organizing for justice created a perfect way to do that!

Start with Relationships

When powerful congregations make their focus developing people, it naturally follows that they don't start out talking about issues. Just as we, as individuals, need to stop talking at people about issues and begin talking with people about our stories and values, our churches need to begin making the same transition. Since our goal is to build a powerful congregation, the core work of our team has to be initiating and deepening our relationships with the members of our church. That's why most organizing efforts kick off not with a major sermon or special educational event, but rather with a congregation-wide listening campaign. Leadership teams spend two to three months focused on one-on-one meetings and group house meetings to build new relationships, identify additional leaders within the congregation, and learn the issues that are in the hearts and affecting the lives of the people within our church.

Powerful churches know that, in the end, the reason people don't take action isn't that they don't know enough; it is that no one in relationship with them has made the effort to invite them and pull them out of the fear/apathy/busyness that keeps most of us from doing what we wish we would do. So we start from relationship. We don't talk about issues until we know what issues our people really care enough to act on. We can only know this through relationship. We don't ask people to serve on a committee until we know their vision for themselves and understand how being in a role can help them grow into that vision. We can only know this by being in relationship with them. We don't ask people to join us for a protest or action until we have first built a relationship and understood their values enough to know that the action is something they care about. That way, when we do decide to take action on an issue, start a new ministry, or make a change in the way we go about our life as the church, we know that we are reflecting the desires of our congregation and community.

When we start from relationship, we don't ask people to do what *we* wish everyone would do. Instead, we ask people to do something we know that they care about. And, finally, someone is invited to take an action, step into a role of leadership, or join us in a new endeavor, they are more likely to say yes when it is coming out of a relationship. Powerful churches make these the standard operating procedures of their work, building everything off of a foundation of relationship.

And this kind of focused relational work doesn't just happen. It is the result of thoughtfully constructing a plan based on the congregation's goals and needs. Listed in the appendix are a few actual planning tools and examples that congregations have used, but to aid your church's planning process, let's think through the questions to answer. Maybe grab a piece of paper or journal and write some notes for each question as you read. Then discuss your thoughts with other members of your team or church.

1. What are your goals for your listening campaign or organizing drive? Whom are you trying to reach? Do you want to build deeper relationships within your church? Identify the issues the members of your congregation are facing? Engage your community outside the walls of your church? Create a deeper sense of the calling to gospel justice within your church?

2. What tool or tools will help you achieve your goals? If you want to build more powerful relationships and call out new leaders, a plan focused on one-on-ones will make sense. If you are really interested in talking to more people in your church about issues, you might start with a month of general house meetings, and then a second month of issue-specific house meetings and one-on-ones with potential new leaders. If you want to engage the broader community, you are going to have to do some canvassing and use your current outreach ministry opportunities.

3. Who will do this? And how many people do you need? Generally, asking people to spend a few hours a week on a drive seems reasonable. So each person can probably average one or two one-on-ones a week, or canvass once a week. House meetings tend to need a few people to coordinate, set a time, and invite people, so having a leader be responsible for one or two in a month tends to work. So if we want to have a hundred one-on-ones in our church over the coming two months, I know that I need at least ten leaders with me on a

team to make sure this happens. Is your team big enough? Is participating in the drive an opportunity for new leaders to test being part of your work?

4. How long will your drive be? And what else will you stop doing to focus on it? Most churches have found that a campaign of between eight and twelve weeks works best. This is enough time to do real work but a short enough time frame to be manageable and not drag on. A season is often a good indicator. Spending the summer on listening to get ready for the ministry year can work. Using the preparation season of Advent or Lent can fit beautifully into the liturgical life of the church. And, since the day doesn't get magically longer, we need to decide what other pieces of church work we will put on the back burner for a few months to truly invest in our congregational organizing. Can you take a break from regular ministry meetings? Can you cancel an event this year and invest the planning time in a listening campaign?

Answering these questions will help you and your congregation shape the organizing drive that you need. Sometimes your drive can simply be one long pattern. There's nothing wrong with doing eight weeks of one-on-ones; in fact, it might be the absolute best thing for your congregation. But drives can often be divided into two stages, often a broader stage and then a more specific one.

For example, one congregation I knew was most interested in understanding the issues their congregation members cared about and calling out new leaders. They decided that the main tool they wanted to use was house meetings because their congregation already had a strong culture of small groups. They divided their drive into two phases of four to five weeks. They recruited a team of sixteen leaders to help lead the drive. In the first half, in teams of two, they held general house meetings with almost their whole congregation. In fact, they set aside a specific Sunday where their pastor agreed to keep the sermon short and to ask the congregation to pair off into house meetings at the end of worship. After these initial house meetings, the team held a halfway-point meeting to address two questions: first, what issues had they learned about; and second, what potential new leaders had they identified for their social justice work or other ministry needs? Half the team then focused on holding four to five issue-specific house meetings around those identified issues with members of the church who had talked about them. The other half held one-on-ones with the potential leaders they had identified in which they explored the person's passion and interest and made a clear proposition for them to step into leadership. At the end of the drive, they held a coffee hour potluck where they reported to the entire congregation on what they had learned and set plans for new actions for the congregation.

This sort of process ensures that we are building our church's capacity to be powerful, and, at the same time, we are clear about how we identify the issues and activities that our congregation will take part in. Especially as our churches begin to move into public action and start getting noticed, it's incredibly common for people to come up and start asking why we are focused on this or that issue, or, even more likely, why we *aren't* focused on their pet issue. In activist congregations, the answer to these questions is often that we focus on the issue that the chair of the social concerns committee cares about, or whatever someone brought to the pastor first. But powerful congregations that start with relationships and develop people have three very clear guidelines.

First, issues come from the church. If we said nothing else, this guideline might still be enough for us. By conducting in-depth listening campaigns, we know the issues people in our congregation and community really care about. Not just the people who speak up first or join committees, but all the people. And not just the issues that people talk about but the ones that really affect their lives and that they are willing to take action on.

Second, build long-term partnerships with churches and organizations. Even the largest church in the world cannot create systemic change all on its own. And almost no congregation has the capacity to do issue and legislative research on every issue it wants to take on. Powerful congregations create long-term partnerships with other churches and with organizations, and these partnerships can help us learn about and clarify some of the issues that we are hearing about within our congregations. Ideally, our churches should be a part of shaping the agendas of the partnerships, through our listening as well.

For more economically comfortable and white congregations, this is even more important. We need to build these long-term partnerships in order to hear from the people most directly affected by injustice about the issues that need to be addressed. Having long-term partnerships across racial, economic, and even geographic lines that help inform our issue selection can ensure that powerful congregations take action based on real needs.

Third, new issues must come with new people. In one very active church I work with, the leadership team found that as they began to get organized and made the shift from activist to powerful, more and more people would come to their Faith in Action team and ask for them to become involved in their own pet issue. The issues were all important, but the team knew they couldn't take on everything. So they decided that for their full committee to take on an issue and make it part of the church's overall social justice work, the issue had to meet three criteria: (1) it had to have come up in a certain number (usually ten) of one-on-ones with congregation members; (2) the person who was bringing the issue forward also had to have at least two other new leaders, that is, people who had not previously been members of the social justice committee; and (3) the person bringing up the issue had to have an outside organization or church to partner with. If a person came to the team and wanted an issue to be acted upon, the committee laid out these guidelines, which encouraged the person to go and build relationships. This way, there was a clear understanding of how an issue got on the church's agenda and a safeguard to protect against the same committed, passionate people taking on more and more work and burning out.

Obviously, this doesn't hold true for things like one-time, emergency responses or mobilizations, but, in the long-term, having a clear set of guidelines by which our congregations and organizations select the issues we work on is a vital component of moving as a powerful church. These may not be the exact criteria that work for you. What criteria will your church use?

And Don't Stop

But the real secret of powerful churches is that they never stop focusing on relationships. And this is the hard part. It's the difference between the zeal of the convert and following a lifelong commitment to our faith; or between the binge dieter who drops fifteen pounds for a wedding but then puts them back on over the next six months and the person who makes lifelong changes and gets healthier. Or, in Jesus's terms, the difference between the seed without root that springs up quickly and then falls away as opposed to the seed that is planted in good soil and yields a harvest one hundredfold.

I've seen many churches decide to make this transition, lead a fantastic listening campaign, build a justice team, and see real results in the newfound power and effectiveness of their congregation. Instead of that same old justice team, they have a larger group that is moving with accountability. They brought twenty-five people out to our first public action when we had never brought more than a handful before! But then the growth slows. A year later, they probably won't have gone back to where they were before, but they haven't expanded either. They've just achieved a new normal, which then slowly begins to decline.

What's happened? We let our relational work slide. I often found that, once I had led a church through these early stages, built a team, done a listening campaign, and begun to take public action, I would get caught up in the excitement of campaigns or the pressure of recruiting new churches and realize that I had not sat down for a one-on-one with a new leader at that church in months. Even my one-on-ones with existing leaders had gone from relational conversations or challenging pushes for growth to task oriented, "let's get the agenda together" check-ins.

The most powerful and effective churches never forget that their work is based in relationship; they therefore maintain a regular relational practice and launch new relational initiatives on a fairly regular basis. Maybe these practices aren't as intensive as the initial listening campaign and organizing push, where members are conducting nothing but one-on-ones, maybe doing one to two a week. They may be scaled back to members of the team doing one relational meeting a month, but, nonetheless, the work of continuing to build and deepen relationships keeps going. And, every year or so, the church does a renewed relational drive. We might focus on a different aspect of our work, maybe a series of one-on-ones with lapsed members or focusing specifically on canvassing our local community outside of our church, but we always remember that at our congregation's core is the relational power that God calls us to.

Engage the Whole Church

No matter how well planned your process is, no matter how well developed and well utilized the members of your leadership team are, in the end, your congregation can't be truly powerful if the whole congregation isn't engaged in the work of justice. Does this mean every member should engage in social justice action? Probably not. But a large number of your congregants should, at least occasionally. More importantly, the work must be talked about and seen as the work of the entire church. Remember how incredibly proud I was of my home church, when, after a few years of organizing, I heard a member I knew, who was not a member of our Faith in Action team or even a particularly politically engaged person, say matter of factly, "Marching and holding politicians accountable is what our church *does*"? This is a person whom, if you met at work or on the porch, you would never mistake for a political activist, and yet, their regular church life now included accountability sessions, trips to the state capitol, and rallies.

Most of our members don't have the time or inclination to become leaders in social justice work. We have jobs. We have families. We don't think of ourselves as political people. And that's okay. Powerful churches recognize that, while we need to develop a number of committed and skilled leaders, we also need to have lower levels of commitment available to engage the entire congregation.

We've already talked about the first, and most key, way to do this. Engage the entire church in the relationship building process. Have one-on-ones with as many people as possible during your listening campaigns. Have "house meetings" with all the different groups and ministries of your congregation. Make sure that you regularly continue to meet with and talk to people outside of the social justice circle.

Another great practice is to have opportunities a few times

a year for the whole church to participate and have things that everyone can do right from the pews. A pastor told me that the church knew what Sunday they celebrated the pastor's anniversary every year and which day of the month they served at the food pantry; so those were on the calendar. He challenged me to build a similar model for our advocacy work. Of course we always want to have people who can drop everything and head to the state capitol to lobby, but that's not realistic for most of our lives (and tends to privilege people without kids and with jobs that provide flexibility). So we made our issues assembly the first Saturday of October that wasn't Columbus Day weekend. We set Martin Luther King Day as our major accountability session and decided to travel to the state capitol on the third Tuesday after Easter every year. That way, the whole church knew about the dates, and people could plan to take a day off work, not schedule another church activity, or skip golf that day. Similarly, asking churches to sign postcards to elected officials during service and hand them in with the offering, or asking everyone to make a quick phone call during coffee hour can be great ways to get the whole church involved in a very simple and accessible action. Of course, we still need to mobilize on different days and on shorter notice, but, having those days on the calendar ensured that a huge percentage of the church was engaging in our justice work. And guess what? When people start doing those three days (because everyone else is) they realize that they like this kind of advocacy, and they become more likely to respond to those other calls to action.

Finally, powerful churches make sure that everyone hears about the justice work. Leadership teams regularly make announcements and have space in the church bulletin. Instead of just announcing upcoming events, we also always report back to the church about our work and let them know what is next. That way, we continue to build a sense of ownership: "This is where we are in the project that we are all working on."

We might say, one Sunday:

"Good morning, church! As you all remember, this summer, along with five of our partner churches in the neighborhood, we did small group meetings in our congregation and canvassed our local community. We learned that a lot of us are really concerned with the attempt to close our local community center. So we are inviting our alderman to our annual legislative public meeting in a few weeks to demand that he keep it open. Now we need everyone to make sure he shows up. Can you sign the postcards in your bulletins and drop them in the collection plate?"

Next week, a different leader announces,

"Good morning, church! Last week we collected over one hundred postcards to the alderman demanding that he attend our meeting in two weeks and commit to keeping our community center open. But when he shows up, he needs to know our whole church is standing together on this issue, so we all need to be there. Please sign up in the back to make sure you're coming!"

And then, on the Sunday after the meeting, a third leader says,

"Good morning again, church! On Thursday night, our annual legislative meeting was a great success. We had a powerful meeting with our alderman. More than fifty of us were present in a crowd of over three hundred! Seeing us all there, the alderman committed to keeping our community center open! We want to make sure he knows that we appreciate it and that we are expecting him to keep his word, so please sign the thank-you card we have in the back, so he knows every member of our church is counting on him!"

With each announcement and action, everyone at your church has an opportunity to contribute, even in a small way.

Our entire congregation is engaged in the effort to move this issue and has a part in winning it!

Stop Meeting to Meet

Try a thought experiment for a minute. Think about the word "meeting." What images come to mind?

Sitting around a table or in front of a presentation while checking our Facebook page, perhaps?

And what emotions do you associate with meetings?

Boredom. Annoyance. Maybe wishing to be somewhere else?

And church meetings are the worst! Usually a prayer, followed by a long stream of reports. Maybe "old business" and then "new business." They never start on time, little gets accomplished, and who knows when they end! No wonder everyone hates meetings!

Now look at your calendar. How many hours a week or a month do you spend in meetings (not counting one-on-ones)? I find that between work and church, I spend at least ten hours a week in meetings. I don't know about you, but I don't have ten hours a week to waste!

For years and years, I have led a three-day organizing training. It covers all sorts of issues: power, one-on-ones, public actions, campaign design, leadership development. But over and over, in the final evaluation, when asked what session was the most impactful, people would say the session on effective meetings! This used to surprise me. I mean, it was a fun session with a role play of a meeting gone horribly wrong, but, really!? More impactful than a session on power analysis or leadership development?

Yet it's true. One of the first things I hear people comment on when they come to an organizing meeting at a powerful church is how different that meeting feels. Powerful churches hold meetings with purpose that get things done, and, consequently, people actually enjoy them! I've met people who have been active in their churches for years, and yet have not really enjoyed church meetings until they began organizing!

No matter how wonderful our one-on-ones are, and no matter how great our ideas for campaigns and actions may be, if we cannot bring people together to make decisions and set plans, we can't move our values forward effectively and powerfully in our world, and our congregations cannot ever become the forces for justice that we dream. So how do we start holding good meetings?

Hold a pre-meeting. If we are going to get people together, we should spend some actual time thinking about what we want to accomplish. For a small meeting, this might just be a "meeting with yourself" or with a co-facilitator. For a major congregational meeting or public meeting, it probably needs to be a full prep session with your leadership team. But, in either case, we need to ask ourselves what we are hoping to accomplish and how we are going to get there.

Set a clear goal. The purpose of a meeting should always be to make a decision or plan a course of action. If the majority of a meeting is taken up just by sharing information, then cancel the meeting. Send the information out, and I'll read it on the train or while I'm waiting to pick my kids up from school. I don't need to come to a meeting for that. Bring people together only to actually get something done.

Have an agenda and a chairperson. Yep! Someone has to be in charge! A chair needs to control the meetings, keep us on task, and make sure we accomplish our goal. Control doesn't mean making all the decisions or doing all the talking, but it does mean ensuring that the meeting is not sidetracked and, yes, sometimes pushing our group to make a decision by cutting people off who are going off topic. And an agenda can't just say, "Opening prayer, old business, new business, and closing prayer." It should lay out, with specific roles and times, what is going to be presented and what decisions will be made.

Start and end on time. I know, for me and my church, this is a tough one. Church folk run on different time! But when we start everything late, and then rehash stuff as people come in, and then run over the time we set, everyone feels annoyed. Moreover, if I show up on time but then wait around for ten minutes before other people mosey in, the next time (if I come back at all) I show up ten minutes late. But then maybe the latecomers, knowing the meeting didn't start until 7:12 last time anyway, don't show up until 7:18! And pretty soon our 7:00 meetings barely start by 7:30 and now run past 9:00! And, eventually, I stop coming. Starting and ending right on time helps everyone understand that we respect everyone's time, are accountable to one another, and are here to get things done. One pastor I know got tired of always starting services late, so he started locking the doors at 9:31 (services started at 9:30) and not opening them again until service was over. Granted, this is a little extreme, but, guess what? The members of his congregation are all there by 9:30, while, at my church, we never start 10:30 Mass at 10:30! There is a shared understanding that everyone will show up, so we don't make people wait; and, from what I can tell, his church appreciates it.

Evaluate and follow up. In organizing we have a saying, "Anything worth doing is worth evaluating." So if the thing we are working on is worth getting everyone together for an hour or an hour-and-a-half meeting, it is worth spending five minutes evaluating if we did a good job and how we can improve our performance. I've found that powerful churches regularly evaluate our meetings and our work to ensure that we get better.

So there you have it! It's not rocket science. Does your church utilize these kinds of best practices?

How do you usually feel coming out of meetings in your congregation? Are you ready to start taking our meetings seriously and making them effective to transform the way our congregations act and move in the world?

Role of the Pastor

Since powerful churches are led by teams of leaders, and not just one person, what is the role of the pastor in the social justice work of a powerful church? Some pastors feel that the work of justice is central to their call and want to be engaged in every aspect of their congregation's organizing. And that's an amazing blessing. But some pastors don't feel as called to the work of justice, or don't have the capacity to be at every meeting of a leadership team. That's okay too. If your pastor isn't the next coming of Dr. King or if you are a pastor who wants your church to be a powerful force for justice but just cannot take on the major leadership of another project, never fear! Your church can still be a powerful one. The pastor doesn't need to be at every meeting and action, but there are some crucial things that they do need to do.

To begin with, pastors need to talk about justice and, in particular, the church's social justice work. This includes preaching about the justice issues your church is working on as well as providing space in terms of the announcements and the bulletin for the church's organizing work. Let's face it; the way most people interact with our church is through Sunday worship, so if the work of justice isn't a part of that worship space and time, it is not central to who your congregation is, and, therefore, your church can't be powerful.

A second key aspect of the pastor's work is about showing up. Not to everything, but to the key moments. Remember those few big times a year that are on the church calendar? Those really need the pastor's presence. If the pastor regularly doesn't show up for actions that are supposed to be church wide, it sends a message that this work is peripheral to the church's identity. For those few times a year, the pastor needs to say, "I'll be there and I hope you will be too!" The other key moment for the pastor to show up is for important meetings with decision makers. As much work as we put into building lay leadership, for most elected officials, pastors represent a different level of church engagement, so for faith-based justice efforts, when it is time to meet with the mayor, we need pastors to show up and bring their moral authority to our cause.

Finally, we need pastors to allow lay leaders to actually lead. There are just too many church meetings for a pastor to be at every one, so we need pastors to allow the lay leaders who make up the social justice team to make decisions and move forward on their own. One other aspect of this means that pastors need to be accessible to the key leaders when they need to get feedback or information in the same way they are accessible to the heads of the finance committee and the deacon's board.

When I meet with pastors, they often say, "I really want this for my church, but I can't lead it." I'll usually say that is fine, but ask for a strong commitment to do three things. Can you speak and preach about these issues, show up five or six times a year, and be accessible to your key lay leaders? If so, there's no reason your church cannot be powerful. If not, then I usually say that, without this minimal level of commitment, a church can't move deeply into justice work, which means we both need to pray about whether or not living out the call to do justice is really going to be a part of our church's ministry. The good news is that, when presented in these terms, almost all pastors can make this commitment.

Take Up the Cross

Moving from being an activist church to a powerful one takes work. We have to change some of our standard operating procedures and maybe even ruffle some feathers. But can we afford not to become powerful?

With racism destroying our lives and communities, with poverty and economic inequality devastating our neighbors, with environmental disasters and climate change threatening our very world, can we afford for our churches merely to give lip service to the work of God's justice or issue statements without any boots on the ground?

When we become powerful, we accept that we are called to make real change happen. St. Teresa of Avila famously said, "God has no hands but yours, no feet but yours. . . . Yours are the feet with which he is to go about doing good. Yours are the hands with which he is to bless his people." When we move as powerful churches, when we can actually act as God's mighty hands, on behalf of God's justice, when we can truly create change rather than just say nice words, we can participate with God in creating God's kingdom. Some of the most powerful moments of closeness to God I have experienced have been while moving with whole churches to transform our communities. When Jesus says, "No one pours new wine into old wineskins" (Mark 2:22), one of the things I think he means is that we must change the way we do things in order to enter into the kingdom. Powerful churches create new wineskins, new structures and systems for our work, so we can hold and create the power God is calling us to.

So ask yourself now, how will you make your church powerful? Who will be a part of your team? How will you focus on building relationships and developing people? And how will the world look different because you did?

PART III

Taking Action for Change

CHAPTER 10

I Came Not to Bring Peace but the Sword

Conflict

Building a powerful congregation, of course, is only half the journey. Once our congregations become powerful, in deep relationship with one another, engaging our whole church and developing new leaders inspired by the call for gospel justice, we actually have to take that power out into the world. We need to wield this power in the service of God's kingdom. And this involves engaging with the powers and principalities of our time. When we do, we face a whole new set of issues. One of the first is our aversion to conflict.

There is no faster way to take the wind out of a faith-based justice effort than to accuse the campaign of being "un-Christian" toward the decision maker who is the target of the effort. In fact, I've regularly seen elected officials do this themselves. A group of faithful activists confront an elected official regarding their position on a key issue, a vote to cut funding for life-saving health care programs or a refusal to stand up against racist sentencing laws, and the official says, "Whoa! Whoa! I thought you were all good Christians. That's why I agreed to meet with you. This isn't how I expect church folks to act!" And the meeting grinds to a halt or the good churchgoers sheepishly apologize. Or you present an upcoming event or ask your pastor or church mission's committee if you can announce an upcoming protest at service on Sunday, and someone says, "That doesn't sound like we are acting very Christ-like toward representative so-and-so," and, to avoid creating dissension within the church, the announcement goes unmade.

People of faith have a real problem with confrontation. So we need to grapple with the following question: when we engage in confrontational tactics or surface tension, are we being un-Christian?

WWJD?

"What Would Jesus Do?" bracelets and other paraphernalia have become so ubiquitous and clichéd that for many they have lost all meaning, but this is still a good place to start. Or, to be more precise, what did Jesus do? What did Jesus say and do in terms of conflict?

The image that we are given most often of Jesus is the prince of peace, a light-skinned, blonde man sitting in an idyllic field lovingly engaging with a group of children and reminding us that "blessed are the meek." Seems pretty clear, right? Jesus would definitely *not* engage in aggressive direct action!

But wait! Is that really what Jesus said and did?

While Jesus does certainly teach us about love for our fellow people, there is another side to his teaching and ministry. My college priest often referred to this side as the Jesus who eats railroad spikes for breakfast.

Just consider the following: As he prepares the twelve disciples to go out on their own, Jesus tells them, "Do not think that I have come to bring peace upon the earth. I have come to bring not peace but the sword" (Matthew 10:34). To go out and proclaim the gospel, in other words, is to raise and incite a great deal of conflict.

Speaking publicly in the temple, Jesus calls out the leaders of the Jewish people for an entire chapter of the Gospel of Matthew, culminating with, "You serpents, you brood of vipers, how can you flee from the judgment of Gehenna?" (Matthew 23:33).

When his own right-hand disciple questions the necessity of confronting the Roman and Jewish authorities, Jesus calls him "Satan," and not just in private: "At this he turned around and, *looking at his disciples*, rebuked Peter and said, 'Get behind me, Satan. You are thinking not as God does, but as human beings do'" (Mark 8:33, my emphasis).

And let's not forget marching into Jerusalem and overturning the moneychangers' tables in the temple! In the account in the Gospel of John, Jesus even uses a whip made of cords. (The scripture is unclear as to whether or not he actually hits anyone with it, but he definitely "drove them all out" [John 2:15].)

So what would Jesus do? Say what you want to about him, but the historical Jesus was not a mild-mannered white man in a field. He was a confrontational, dark-skinned Palestinian who did not shy away from a fight. He very directly and publicly confronted any system or person in opposition to the kingdom of God that he was proclaiming, a kingdom based on God's justice and radical care for those at the bottom of the social order. His ministry begins by offending the powerful in a synagogue to the point that they try to throw him off a cliff (Luke 4:29) and ends with his confrontational march into Jerusalem and the cleansing of the temple. Confrontation is, in fact, a fairly central part of Jesus's ministry.

And that's just Jesus! Moses and the Old Testament prophets are even more confrontational, especially toward those in power. Moses calls down plagues and even death on the Egyptians when Pharaoh refuses to act with justice and free the enslaved Jewish people. The prophets continually confront, challenge, and condemn the rulers for unjust treatment of the poor and marginalized. Over and over God's chosen spokespeople defiantly and publicly challenge unjust rulers.

To Love or Be Nice?

"But wait!" comes the voice of the skeptic, "Doesn't Jesus also tell us to love our enemies and turn the other cheek?"

He certainly does. But we cannot use these lines to wiggle out of the clear call to confront injustice. In fact, this teaching isn't about avoiding conflict or angry feelings at all; it is a tactical teaching on how we, as Christians, are supposed to engage in nonviolent direct action. Don't think so? Stick with me.

First of all, we should be clear about what Jesus does not say, because we often get confused. Jesus doesn't say that we shouldn't have enemies. In fact, telling people to "love your enemies" presupposes that we have them. Jesus is a straight shooter and says what he means pretty clearly. If we weren't supposed to have enemies, he would have just said that. But Jesus knows that following him means we have to engage and confront injustice and come into conflict with the supporters and leaders of unjust systems. People who are advocating for a vision of the world directly opposed to God's kingdom of compassion and justice will oppose us. We will have enemies, and we must reject the evil and injustice that they do. At the same time, we must remain open to them as human beings and refuse to hate them.

Similarly, while Jesus tells us to love our enemies, he does not tell us to like them or be nice to them. And thank God! Because that would be truly impossible. As I've become a parent, I've come to understand this distinction even more deeply. Every Saturday morning, my kids know they have to clean their rooms before we can go to swimming class at the local pool. My daughter is a good cleaner and generally gets her room done. My son is in a particularly stubborn phase, where he often refuses to clean his room. And sometimes this means he doesn't get to go to swimming. Of course, as my daughter gets changed and heads out the door, he throws himself on the floor demanding to go. "You're mean!" he shouts at me. "I don't like you! I'm not your friend!" And, like so many parents before me, I explain that it's not my job to be his friend; it is my job to help him grow up to be a responsible, moral human being. Which means no swimming that day. Loving my son does not mean "being nice" or not making him deal with the consequences of his actions. In fact, if I didn't teach my son that he must fulfill his responsibilities and that his actions have consequences, I would not be doing a good job as his parent.

Every parent understands this distinction, but we seem to forget it in so many other areas of our life. We confuse being loving and Christ-like with being nice and avoiding conflict. Loving our enemies means honoring their personhood, refusing to do them harm, and refusing to do violence, but it does not extend to protecting their feelings or allowing them to continue to perpetrate injustice that harms others. Love also means speaking harsh truths to people, especially to those in power.

One of the leaders I've been deeply privileged to work with is Rev. Cy Fields, the pastor of New Landmark Missionary Baptist Church in Chicago. Pastor Fields shared his story of engaging in confrontation:

As a clergy leader I found myself fueled with righteous indignation to demand that the city get serious about reforming a police department that has a storied history of excessive abuse and negative interactions with African American and other communities of color. For over a year our team of pastors, community leaders, parents, and organizers met at local congregations with other concerned residents.  *We held large public demonstrations, church rallies, and met with local aldermen. Our actions indeed garnered the mayor's attention and led to meetings with him, only to have them end with cool pleasantries, firm handshakes, and empty promises to meet again, again, and again. With an underground buzz about the release of the LaQuan McDonald tape that would reveal a CPD officer killing a teenager with sixteen shots as he walked away from the police, many of us felt that the moment was urgent and we needed more than just words this time!*

Just prior to the release of the tape we met with the mayor at City Hall again. We were poised in expressing our disappointment about his indifference toward police reform, and we spoke truth in presenting our demands. We had decided in advance that if the mayor remained intransigent we would end the meeting. And as the meeting progressed, we were hearing the same empty rhetoric and refusal to take concrete action. As chair of the meeting the decision was up to me. I stood up, abruptly rejecting the mayor's words and saying that if he was unwilling to commit to real action there was no reason to keep talking. In unison our delegation walked out, thus ending the meeting. A bold move for a group of faith believers unsure of the repercussions.

In strategizing on our future plans we decided that a more impactful demonstration was needed to show the mayor, CPD, and city council that justice for Chicago residents could not be delayed nor denied. Our decision was to hold a bolder faith-in-action protest against the mayor. We believed blood was on the administration's hands.

We descended on the mayor's office with a large group of churchgoers. There was something divine about hearing an early morning crowd who the previous Sunday sang praises in a church pew but on this day was thunderously chanting on the Chicago's fifth-floor political sanctuary called City Hall. Clergy and everyday church members, with their hands covered with red paint, broke through the linked arms of the police line and plastered their hand prints on the doors of the mayor's office. The red hands on the doors symbolized the bloodshed in the streets at the hands of corrupt police officers that was now on the hands of the mayor. As many of our Faith in Action team members were being arrested, others were kneeling in prayer; some were singing and shouting, sprawled out on the floor and waving signs demanding change. The Spirit was with us as we pleaded for change and confronted the political powers for justice and reform.

For some, this might seem radical or un-Christian. In my sixteen years of pastoring, dozens of well-meaning people have asked me, "Why are you into politics? Aren't you a pastor?" I don't view actions calling for social justice, equity, and accountability as being a politician. I've come to understand that the cross of Christ calls for justice. Just as there was conflict in the crucifixion scene that changed the world, at times confrontation is also a necessary action in order to change a community, eliminate an unjust policy, or dissuade an elected official from following the status quo. Then there's an ancillary drive to prove to political leaders and our local residents that Westside clergy and churches can have influence when we work together. I know I am charged to stand and represent a moral voice even if it means direct confrontation.

Our efforts over a two-year period came to a climax. The actions of people who worship on Sunday and fought for justice on Monday contributed to the eventual agreement between the U.S. Department of Justice and the city of Chicago to make improvements in CPD after their report concluded that CPD possessed a culture of "excessive violence."

Dr. Cornel West said, "It's a beautiful thing to be on fire for justice."

This sort of direct action feels scary and uncomfortable to many of us. But Jesus never calls us to comfort. And when we refuse to take public action and confront those who perpetrate injustice, what we really do is put concern for the feelings of the oppressor and our own unwillingness to step out of our comfort zones above the needs of the people and communities for whom we are advocating. In Pastor Fields's story, the Chicago police were quite literally killing young men of color, with impunity, because of a complete lack of structural oversight of police misconduct. Suggesting that the mayor didn't know about these issues strains belief; there had been numerous reports on the subject, and his own budget was paying out millions of dollars each year in settlements for police misconduct. We had requested meetings through more traditional, collegial methods and been rebuffed. So we could either take more aggressive action or simply allow this abuse to continue in our neighborhoods. It would have been easier or more comfortable to let it rest, but to do so would have been to abandon the very people for whom we are called to care. In the end, the question is not, What would Jesus do? We know the answer; he would march into Jerusalem, or city hall, or the New York Stock Exchange and confront those who perpetrate and perpetuate injustice. The question is, are we willing to follow Jesus and put our demands for justice and our love for our communities and the oppressed ahead of our own personal comfort and the feelings of the people who are doing the oppressing?

God's Playbook for Conflict

If we are ready to engage in constructive conflict on behalf of God's justice, there are some very clear guideposts that Jesus and the prophets give us for confronting power.

Nonviolence

While loving our enemies does not prohibit us from confronting the perpetrators of injustice, it does place a pretty clear prohibition on the use of violence. When Jesus is confronted by an unjust arrest that will surely lead to death, he refuses to allow his disciples to respond with violence: "Put your sword back into its sheath, for all who live by the sword will die by the sword. Do you think that I cannot call upon my Father and he will not provide me at this moment with more than twelve legions of angels (Matthew 26:52-53)?" He even heals the servant who has had his ear severed! Clearly Jesus has the power to respond with overpowering force, but he refuses to do so.

Even more famous, of course, is Christ's teachings on retaliation in the Sermon on the Mount:

> You have heard it said, "An eye for an eye and a tooth for a tooth." But I say to you, offer no resistance to one who is evil. When someone strikes you on the right cheek, turn the left to him as well. If anyone wants to go to law with you over your tunic, hand him your cloak as well. Should anyone press you into service for one mile, go with him for two miles. (Matthew 5:38-41)

These powerful teachings clearly call us to refuse to engage in violence, but, at the same time, they are also powerful, even subversive, lessons in how to not back down in the face of violence and oppression, and even to turn the power of violence back on itself through creative, nonviolent direct action. Gandhi and King used this teaching as the centerpiece of their strategies to confront injustice, by standing up to violence and denying the oppressor's power. Theologian Walter Wink in his seminal works on power and nonviolence in the scripture provides a deeper analysis of how truly radical and subversive these teachings were, given the context of Jesus's time; each one, in fact, is a guideline for incredibly powerful direct action that turns power relationships on their head!

Wink explains that, in Jesus's time, the right hand was what was used for public interaction (the left was unclean, and used for cleaning oneself). So how would a person using their right hand strike a person who was facing them on that person's right cheek? With a back-handed blow of course! The appropriate way for a superior to put an inferior in their place. But now imagine that "inferior" person turning their left cheek to the supposed "superior." How do you strike it? You cannot use your left hand,

and to strike with your right hand, you would have to throw a normal punch. But a normal punch is reserved for fights between equals. To strike the left cheek, the supposed superior person would have to acknowledge the supposed inferior as an equal. In this one simple motion, the entire power dynamic has been changed. Instead of being "put in their place" by a backhand slap, the previously downtrodden person has defanged the power of violence and left the oppressor in a quandary, confused and humbled.

Jesus's teaching on being sued for one's tunic creates the same kind of nonviolent reversal. There are two important things to understand here. First, only a very poor person would have to put their very clothes up for collateral; and second, looking on a naked person in Jesus's time brought shame on the person who was doing the looking. So again, we can picture the scenario: a downtrodden, poor person is brought to court to be humiliated by an unjust economic system, forced to remove their outer tunic and hand it over to a much wealthier person. But let's face it, even the tunic probably doesn't pay the full debt. So the person goes further, "No, no, you're right, Mr. Landlord! I have to pay my full debt, so here, take my cloak and my underwear too." With one audacious move, the tables are turned! Now the landlord is sputtering and trying to avert his eyes, as the debtor, completely naked, presses their undergarments into his hands. The landlord would probably push the clothes back and rush away, embarrassed, while all the other debtors in court, awaiting their turn for humiliation, laugh out loud and are suddenly eager to be called forward!

Or finally, we think of "going the extra mile" as a good thing, but not if you were grabbed and forced to carry a soldier's heavy gear. This was a regular experience for the poor Judean peasants in Jesus's audience. The Roman soldiers, who occupied Israel, had to carry a lot of gear. They would often impress local people to carry it for them, so they could stay fresh for fighting (we see a similar situation when Simon of Cyrene is pressed into service by the Roman soldiers to help carry Jesus's cross). But, and this is a big one, to avoid creating too much resentment in the local population, the Roman army had a rule that a soldier could force someone to carry his gear *only for one mile!* And Roman military discipline involved severe punishment for soldiers breaking any rule. So once again, imagine if this happened! A soldier demands some lowly peasant carry his gear, and, after a mile, is prepared to take it back. But instead, the peasant refuses and keeps on walking. Now it is the soldier who is in trouble! If the peasant keeps going, the soldier can get beaten or whipped! Now the soldier is in the ridiculous position of begging the peasant to give back his heavy pack! Through strategic and nonviolent tactics, once again the tables have been turned.

These teachings have been used over and over again to win justice, from Gandhi's movement for Indian independence and the American civil rights movement to nonviolent movements against the USSR. Nonviolent, direct-action strategies have proven their effectiveness when used with the same kind of courage, shrewdness, and creativity that Jesus describes. These kinds of tactics confront the perpetrator of injustice directly with the effects of their actions, while creating a crisis of conscience both in the oppressor and in society at large. At the same time, they are empowering for people who have been beaten down, as they realize that they do have a voice after all and they can leave the powerful dumbfounded. Imagine what powerful actions we could have created during the foreclosure crisis using these models—a caravan of trailers going to the corporate headquarters or the home of the president of the major banks and handing over not just their keys but their clothes and their children's toys as well, unmasking the injustice of the situation. We are not called to submit to injustice but to refuse to use the evil tools of violence and, instead, turn systems of oppression on their heads!

Escalation

But very few of us are ready, upon first hearing about an issue of injustice, to jump to the front of a huge march ready to be met by fire hoses or to strip naked in a public courthouse! The good news is that very few campaigns start this way! So don't panic, because here is what Jesus says:

> If your brother or sister sins against you, go and tell them their fault between you two alone. If they listen, you have won over your brother or sister. If not, take one or two others along with you so that "every fact may be established on the testimony of two or three witnesses." If they refuse to listen to them, tell the church. If they refuse to listen even to the church, treat them as you would a Gentile or a tax collector. (Matthew 18:15-17)

The principle here is escalation. We begin our campaigns quietly, often by attempting to meet with decision makers in small groups and by using fairly nonconfrontational tactics, such as letter-writing campaigns. But as decision makers refuse to listen and create change, our actions become increasingly public and confrontational. While we continue to love our enemies, pray for them, and remain open to them as human beings, we also must continue to bring an ever louder public witness to the injustice they are perpetrating. Jesus goes so far as to call for casting such a person out of the community ("treat them as you would a Gentile").

In Rev. Fields's testimony earlier in this chapter, we did not wake up one morning, realize there was a problem with police brutality, and march on the mayor's office to put bloody handprints on his door. Instead, after hearing dozens of stories from members of our churches and communities about being abused and violated by the police, our leadership teams had engaged in deep research to come up with a series of needed reforms. And then we did what this Gospel says we should. A few pastors sent a cordial letter to the mayor asking to meet and discuss the issue. They got no response. So more people called and emailed the office. And got no response again. Then we went to the church(es) and thousands of people of faith sent postcards to the mayor calling for him to meet with us and take action on police reform. But he still refused to meet. So we began a series of direct actions, culminating in bringing the vision of the police violence faced by people in our neighborhoods every day right to the fifth floor of city hall and all the television cameras as the mayor was running for re-election. And this pressure eventually convinced him that he had to meet with us to begin to confront this issue.

Properly escalating actions allows decision makers an opportunity to do the right thing early on, before facing public criticism. It also allows people in our churches to come along with us. As they learn about an issue, they may be willing to sign a postcard or make a phone call about it. As they see that there is no response or that the decision maker still refuses to do the right thing, they may then be willing to join a delegation to their office. As they see that there is still no response, they may be ready to go even further. At each stage, we offer the decision maker the chance to do what is right while being steadfast in knowing that, if they refuse, we will escalate our call for justice until it finally happens.

Public Actions

In the end, most campaigns around significant justice issues will need to escalate into some sort of public action. As much as we would like for people just to do the right thing based on reasoned argument and goodwill, we know that the conflict Jesus talked about will need to go public eventually to urge decision makers to change their position. The two most common ways we take public action are through direct actions and accountability sessions.

Accountability sessions are some of the most exciting and radical spaces we can create, holy spaces for tension, witness, and covenant. At their core, they involve bringing a decision maker before an organized community and holding them accountable by asking for a clear, yes or no commitment to a specific ask.

Nehemiah 5: 7-13

One of the best biblical accounts of something akin to an accountability session can be found in the book of Nehemiah. After bringing the Jewish people together, returning many to Jerusalem and rebuilding the walls, thus restoring the city, Nehemiah hears the complaints of many people that their own leaders are bleeding them dry by charging interest on loans, a practice that is forbidden. What does Nehemiah do?

> I pondered them in my mind and then accused the nobles and officials. I told them, "You are charging your own people interest!" So I called together a large meeting to deal with them and said: "As far as possible, we have bought back our fellow Jews who were sold to the Gentiles. Now you are selling your own people, only for them to be sold back to us!" They kept quiet, because they could find nothing to say.
>
> So I continued, "What you are doing is not right. Shouldn't you walk in the fear of our God to avoid the reproach of our Gentile enemies? I and my brothers and my men are also lending the people money and grain. But let us stop charging interest! Give back to them immediately their fields, vineyards, olive groves and houses, and also the interest you are charging them—one percent of the money, grain, new wine and olive oil."
>
> "We will give it back," they said. "And we will not demand anything more from them. We will do as you say."

Then I summoned the priests and made the nobles and officials take an oath to do what they had promised. I also shook out the folds of my robe and said, "In this way may God shake out of their house and possessions anyone who does not keep this promise. So may such a person be shaken out and emptied!"

At this the whole assembly said, "Amen," and praised the LORD. And the people did as they had promised.

There are a couple very powerful things here. After an investigation that leads to a clear understanding that an injustice is being perpetrated by the rich against the poor, Nehemiah calls a large public meeting to confront the decision makers. This ensures both that he demonstrates to them that the people are behind him and in addressing the issue engages all of the people who have been wronged. Next, he brings a clear complaint and demand to the nobles and officials: stop charging interest and repay what you have taken. And, most importantly, he gets a clear answer. And not just an answer. He brings forward the priests to formalize the commitment and turn it into a covenant promise. Then he brings the entire crowd into the action. All the people formalize the commitment that has been made by saying "Amen." The officials keep their promise because they have made a covenant with an entire community of people who are ready to hold them accountable.

Organized people of faith today continue to hold accountability sessions as one of the key techniques of faith-based organizing. After careful research of an issue and an escalating set of actions, we ask a decision maker to come before our communities and make a clear commitment, just like Nehemiah did. What I love most about accountability sessions is that they are one of the most concrete examples I have seen of truly living Jesus's teaching that the last shall be first and the first shall be last; they entirely subvert the power relationships in our society. Traditionally, agendas are set and meetings are called at the convenience and on the terms of the powerful. They control who will speak and for how long, what questions will be asked and what answers will be deemed acceptable. In an accountability session, we reverse these dynamics. Church and community groups choose the issues most important to them and set the agenda. We decide who will speak, and, instead of asking decision makers to make long speeches about vague proposals, we ask them direct questions and have them respond with a simple yes or no. A yes answer brings us into a new covenant relationship, moving toward God's kingdom together, while a no demonstrates that they are not yet willing to repent and stand on the side of justice; and therefore, we must continue to escalate our powerful, nonviolent direct action until they are moved.

A number of years ago, I was working with a coalition that was aiming to address violence in our neighborhoods by reducing the amount of time and money the county spent holding nonviolent people in jail before their trials (in other words, people who had not been found guilty of a crime) and instead investing money and diverting people into community-based restorative justice peace hubs that can help turn negative behavior around, repair harm, and heal our communities. One of the key decision makers was the chief judge of the county, Judge Timothy Evans, who controlled the workings of bond court, as well as the creation and implementation of any diversion program or specialty court. Judge Evans had been involved in Chicago politics for decades and was a well-revered figure among many clergy; but, he was also the person who could make the changes that our communities desperately needed. After a series of escalating actions we finally called a public accountability session with the judge.

I was nervous. I had never heard of Judge Evans attending an accountability session before. He was much more likely to attend a fancy luncheon and give long speeches than to actually commit to a concrete plan for reform. Even in our meetings, he had proven very hard to pin down or accept any responsibility.

We always made sure to invite our members to arrive half an hour before the decision maker, and members from the various churches began to fill the sanctuary. Before the judge arrived, one of the pastors who was leading the action explained the long road we had taken to arrive and went over the agenda. And then the choir started singing and that church started to rock (and I started to pray, "Dear God! Let him show up! Touch his heart and move him to do the right thing").

When the judge arrived and was escorted down the center aisle, there were more than five hundred people packing every inch of that church! Several community members movingly shared their experiences and desires, and then it came time for covenant and commitment. First, our entire group stood up and committed to stand with and support judges who took the courageous steps we were asking for. And then, the whole congregation as one made three sets of simple yes or no asks of the judge. Confronted with such moving testimony, clear recommendations, and unity in the audience, the judge committed to each one! And, to seal our new covenant, he and key leaders from our organizations signed a huge scroll signifying our commitments! As he left, the judge said to me, "I had never been to something like this before, but it was just the way you all said it would be!" We had a new relationship of respect and accountability.

Now it wasn't all roses from there, but today on the West Side of Chicago Cook County is opening up the first-ever restorative justice court; new tools are helping to ensure that people are not held meaninglessly in jail simply because they are poor and cannot afford bail, and new money is being invested into neighborhood peace hubs. And many of these changes were pushed forward because of that accountability session in that

West Side church! I don't think that was a particularly comfortable setting for the judge, and, confronting him wasn't easy for many of our members as well, either because of the respect they had for him for his years of service or because of the power he held, especially over people who have had contact with the criminal justice system. But by standing together, reversing the power relationships, and being willing to engage in conflict, our churches were able to drive real change.

Jesus called his disciples to march into Jerusalem and confront the unjust and oppressive systems of Roman occupation and religious collaboration on the part of Jewish leaders. Today the names have changed, but our world is still rife with rulers who put the interests of the wealthy over the needs of the poor, who maintain racist systems, who attack people for being different, and place profits over the needs of people and a healthy planet.

Are we willing to follow Jesus's call and march into the halls of power, wherever they are? Are we willing to let go of our need for comfort and the concern for the feelings of the powerful, to truly stand on the side of gospel justice? Are we ready to be called un-Christian in order to truly follow Christ?

CHAPTER 11

Known by Our Fruits

The World as It Is

For every tree is known by its own fruit. For people do not gather figs from thorns, nor do they gather grapes from a bramble bush. A good person out of the good treasure of their heart brings forth good. —Luke 6:44-45

As we accept our call to become powerful agents of the gospel, to organize people and organize money to move kingdom values forward in the world, we have to move away from the safe security of just "being right" and instead be willing to take responsibility to co-create a more just world with God.

When I graduated from college, I decided to spend a year as a member of the Jesuit Volunteer Corps, a young adult ministry of the Catholic Church, where JVs (as we were called) spend a year living simply together in intentional community, with each working in different justice or charitable ministries. My work was with the Tennessee Coalition to Abolish State Killing (TCASK; now Tennesseans for Alternatives to Capital Punishment) to help advance the work of abolishing the death penalty in the state. I was excited and energized. For years, I had been convinced that for the state to kill, to engage in vengeance, violated the deepest principles of my faith. I had read Sister Helen Prejean's amazing book, *Dead Man Walking,* and been thrilled as Pope John Paul II and the US Conference of Catholic Bishops had called for an end to the death penalty as a part of a seamless garment of life. I believed that we needed to take the teaching seriously that every person was created in the image and likeness of God, which meant that we could never cut off the possibility of redemption or end the life of a human being.

But then I realized that many in the abolition movement had made a strategic move to highlight and advocate for alternatives to capital punishment, most notably life without the possibility of parole (or LWOP). There had been a number of exciting victories, and several states had actually abolished the death penalty, replacing death sentences with LWOP.

Now I was in trouble. You see, I found that LWOP bumped up against my values as well. Didn't I believe that all people were capable of redemption? Most murders are committed by people in their twenties or early thirties. People as young as seventeen are subject to these laws. Were we really saying that we supported a law that said that there was no hope for redemption, repentance, and forgiveness for people, even if they lived another fifty, sixty, or seventy years? That didn't track with what I believed, and I found myself questioning whether I could, in good conscience, join this effort.

I remember praying about this for several weeks. "God, I believe you sent me here, but how can I do this immoral thing?" I knew there were lots of people who agreed with me. In fact, some had stopped working with TCASK because they said they could not support a strategy that did not stand firm in its call for full and complete abolition (they also objected to a strategy that called for a moratorium, a pause, and study of the death penalty, as opposed to full and immediate abolition). Maybe God had sent me here to help lead the abolition movement back to the side of pure truth, I thought. And then God slapped me in the face, as God so often does.

I met the brother of someone who had been executed who would never get to hear his brother's voice again. I met a mother whose son was sitting on death row who had to wake up every day wondering if some faceless judge or court bureaucracy would set a date for her to watch her son die in front of her. I imagined my conversation with them: "I understand that you want to save your son's life and that having him alive, even behind bars, is so much better than losing him forever, but my conscience won't allow me to participate in that effort."

I realized my prayers hadn't been about standing in solidarity with the least of these at all; I had been praying to protect my own sense of moral authority and purity. I was more interested in being 100 percent right than in actually serving the people I was being called to serve.

I had been placed in a position of enormous responsibility for a twenty-two-year-old, entrusted by an organization to help stop an immoral policy of killing people; and I was spending more time on my own hang-ups than in what the real people in front of me actually needed.

Yes! In a perfect world, we could go right from having capital punishment to no death penalty, no LWOP, and a restorative justice paradigm for our entire criminal justice system, but that is simply not the way that the real world works. By insisting on that level of absolutism and perfectionism, I was constraining the chance to make change happen. Forced to confront my own self-righteousness, I realized a hard truth; we have to deal with the world as it is, not the world as we want it to be. True moral leadership calls us to live in the tension between those two worlds; dealing with the world as it is and slowly making choices to transform the world into God's kingdom of justice.

Moving with power requires us to fight for change in sometimes small and infuriating ways. It requires us to engage with, and be accountable to, real people in the real world, even when they frustrate us or puncture our sense of importance. Here are three ways God has continued to challenge me, slapping me out of my certitude to move from activist to powerful.

1. Stop preaching to the choir and reject purity codes

In Mark 9:39-41, Jesus's disciple John comes to him and tells him he saw a man driving out demons in Jesus's name and that he tried to stop him since he wasn't a member of their group. Clearly John was expecting a pat on the back, even though he was trying to stop someone from healing the afflicted. But, we know the story. Jesus says to his disciples: "Do not stop him, for no one who does a miracle in my name can in the next moment say anything bad about me, for whoever is not against us is for us. Truly I tell you, anyone who gives you a cup of water in my name because you belong to the Messiah will certainly not lose their reward."

This Gospel story always struck me as a little silly. How could the disciples be so foolish? Who would try to stop someone from doing good deeds? We can almost hear Jesus say, "Are you nuts!?"

Several years ago, I found myself having a discussion with a pastor of a Baptist church about an upcoming coalition meeting. At the time, our cohort of urban churches had identified the need to address violence, and especially to stem the flow of illegal guns into our communities, as a major area of our work. Our past experience had told us that moving these issues in the Illinois General Assembly was difficult. While we could always count on the votes of the African American legislators along with some liberals who represented other sections of Chicago and the immediate suburbs as well as a few smaller downstate cities, those representatives together didn't make up a majority of the legislature. This meant that we needed to move those legislators from the next ring of more affluent, mostly white suburbs.

On this particular day, I was excited because we had found a way to create a partnership with another faith-based advocacy organization and several denominations made up of people from those very districts who, motivated by their faith, were ready to push their own legislators around the issues identified by our churches. I felt like we could see a real path to victory.

But the pastor shook his head. "I can't work with those groups," he told me.

I was stunned. Hadn't he told me how many parents in his congregation wouldn't even let their kids play outside for fear of a stray bullet? Hadn't he shared how much it hurt him to preside at the funerals of young people and to have to console grieving parents? I had to ask him what the problem was.

"That group is a gay group," he told me. Now I understood what he meant. These churches had taken strong positions in support of gay marriage during the previous year, and they belonged to denominations that were far to the left of the National Baptist Convention on LGBTQ issues. But these churches weren't asking him to advocate for those issues or share their stance. They had agreed to add their political muscle to ours and work on an issue that was of key concern for our churches. And I was pretty sure that we couldn't win this campaign without support in those key swing districts. So I swallowed hard and said, "Pastor, I respect where you are coming from, but I also know how much you have told me that this gun violence is affecting your church and neighborhood. And we both know that this is an uphill fight. Now these people are willing to use their power to support your community, and they aren't asking you to agree with them or even have any discussion about LGBTQ issues. Are you really willing to lose this chance to stop some of these guns from coming onto our streets because of what these folks believe about a completely different issue?"

I'm happy to say that, in this case, we were able to work past it and, in the end, help to pass several bills that placed stronger restrictions on illegal gun sales (selling guns to people who are legally banned from having them). And we needed every one of those suburban churches to do it, too! But it still scares me to think how close we came to not building the coalition of churches that we needed.

This isn't an isolated instance. One denominational leader told me they couldn't join an interfaith prayer vigil to protect social services that meant life or death for literally tens of thousands of people, even though they supported the issue, because their denomination did not believe in praying with others who did not share every one of their doctrinal beliefs!

As people of faith ready to become powerful actors for justice in the world, we need to be serious about God's call to us to actually create change, and not just feel good about ourselves for our advocacy. We need to stop preaching to the choir, get beyond our comfort zones, and engage with people even if they don't share all our beliefs.

Ask yourself, are there groups you refuse to work with? Have you ever been unwilling to join an organization or effort because it wasn't faith based? Or refused to work with groups that engaged the political process because "no candidate is perfect"? Are some groups, especially of directly affected people, "too aggressive" or "too angry" for you?

Jesus's entire mission was about pushing people to get beyond their own comfort zone, their own sense of what they wanted God to be, and to become radical actors for God's kingdom. He asks Peter to step out of the boat onto stormy waves. He marches right into the heart of Jerusalem. He insists that to follow him, his disciples must literally give up everything and not look back. We cannot follow his example if we refuse to engage beyond our own sphere.

So why not go meet with one of those groups you won't work with, or attend one of their events, right now.

2. *Make real change—reject all-or-nothing thinking*

"But that's not enough, we also have to talk about. . . ." How many times have you heard that sentence?

It seems to me that I've heard it in every single discussion about issues in every single community in every single church basement I have ever sat in. There are so many problems and they seem so big that we feel like we need to address them all. And as long as we are just lone voices in the wilderness, moving without power, that may be fine. But as soon as we commit to becoming powerful agents of God's kingdom, we have to engage the world, and that means rejecting all-or-nothing dynamics.

What happens if we try to take on everything at once? We get nothing done. And all the people who have signed up to be a part of our effort get discouraged and leave because very few people want to be a part of a church, organization, or campaign that is more interested in cataloguing and harping about every single problem than with making actual progress.

Try holding a roundtable discussion on violence or education, and just wait. I promise your group will start saying, well, yes, we need more funding in our schools, but we also need to discuss teacher accountability, and we need to address what is happening at home with these kids, and we need to address the violence in our communities, and things were different before they took God out of schools and. . . . All of a sudden, you have a multipronged effort to fix everything wrong with our society in one fell swoop!

In dealing with the world as it is, we have to be willing to take things one at a time. Identify the most pressing concern or concerns, and deal with them; then take on what's next. My mentor, the Rev. Calvin S. Morris, taught me this using the words of an old Baptist hymn, "Yield not to temptation, for yielding is sin. Each victory will aid you, some others to win."

But even when we have agreed to focus on a few key issues, we face pitfalls. Especially as people of faith, we can be so committed to the cause that we are unwilling to compromise or agree to half measures. We know how important the issue is, and we have a beautiful vision of what God's kingdom looks like; so we want it all now!

And this happened in real life to a dear friend of mine, Katelyn Johnson, the executive director of Action Now in Chicago:

Over the past seventeen years, I have spent a lot of time unlearning what I thought I knew about the way the world should be. Growing up, I thought you could either be rich or you could be poor. "Working poor" was a foreign concept and a seeming contradiction, even though that described my family's situation perfectly. We were poor enough to be on welfare; but after my par-

ents worked us off it, we still struggled to make ends meet because my mom made minimum wage, which was just enough to survive. I remember the food stamps, I remember hearing my parents talk about shut-off notices, but I also remember that my mom wasn't around much because she had to work incredibly hard. In 2015, I was blessed to help lead a historic campaign to raise the minimum wage in Chicago as part of the broader "Fight for 15" movement. I found myself reflecting a lot on my childhood. We demanded a true living wage of $15 an hour (up from $8.25, a poverty-level wage in a major city). But as the campaign gained momentum, the mayor cut a deal with the business lobby and launched a counterproposal for a minimum wage that would rise gradually over several years to $13 an hour.

For some in our coalition, it was a no-brainer to accept the deal. For others in the coalition, it was a slap in the face because "the purity of the demand" was for $15 an hour. It was excruciating for me to consider accepting this "compromise." I remember thinking, "Wow, $13 an hour is still a big jump. It would provide *a huge benefit to the economic realities of hundreds of thousands of families just like mine. But it still is not enough to truly raise a family on, especially in Chicago." In the end, I voted to accept the compromise because I knew it would be a significant increase and that the low-income families I worked with couldn't afford to wait years longer for a raise. I knew we'd be able to keep fighting for $15 another day.*

Almost immediately, I was called a sell-out by some of my allies. I understood where they were coming from. I knew that the corporations could afford the $15-an-hour demand. But I knew that we weren't going to win anything above the $13 level, and, not accepting that could mean we won nothing. But, I didn't live up to some people's "justice purity" standards. I tried to share my story with many of my "allies," but they were so convinced of their own righteousness that they could not see my perspective. I also couldn't help but notice that almost always those slinging the muck were people who weren't even impacted by a minimum wage. To me, we won because, prior to our campaign, no one, not the mayor, the city council, or the media were even talking about raising the minimum wage; but I never forgot what it felt like to be called a "sell-out." It hurt more than words could express. Losing $15 hurt me too, but it hurt more to have my allies betray me because I wasn't holding out for perfection. I felt it impossible to build power and win real change for real people only in service of perfection. To this day, some of those people refuse to work with me because I am "soft."

Katelyn understood that demanding absolute victory often means we get nothing. We can undercut our progress and hurt our allies. Even the great social movements won their victories a chunk at a time. Each victory brings real change to the lives of some of God's people, and it inspires members of organizations to keep on marching to the promised land because they see progress!

When have you walked away from a table because people were "too willing to compromise"? Have you ever called an ally a sell-out (even just in your head)? Can you think of anyone in the justice world that you feel morally superior to? Are you refusing to accept the responsibilities of power and make real change?

3. Move in uncertainty

When Jesus called James and John, they were sitting in their boat, fishing with their father. All Jesus told them was to come follow him, and they immediately left their father in the boat and joined him. Joining in a justice effort can be scary. Visiting a legislator's office, attending a rally, or speaking in public about an issue may be very new experiences for the members of your congregation. And one of the first things we often do when confronted with an uncomfortable or unfamiliar situation is to claim that we don't know enough and need to do more research.

Now before anyone gets the wrong idea, I want to be clear that I'm not suggesting that we go off half-cocked or that we shouldn't get our facts straight. Doing our research has to be a part of any campaign. But, more often than not, we use the excuse that we don't know enough to mask the more underlying fact: we don't want to do something this new or uncomfortable.

I learned this fact most clearly when working with a set of Unitarian churches. The Unitarian Church is probably the most progressive denomination in the country, and these congregations were no exception. They had a deep commitment to justice, preached about it constantly, held educational forums at least once a month, gave half their offerings every Sunday to different mission organizations, the whole bit. However, one of the central tenets of the church is also to respect every person's "individual search for truth." So, when it was time to take direct action, the congregational leaders told us over and over again that they couldn't get people to come out.

"Our members say they don't know enough about the issue to commit to being there," they would say. Or they would report that a member asked them a highly technical question about a piece of legislation or a demand we were making, and the leader would feel sheepish about not knowing and not even ask them to come out. Sometimes congregation members would meet with their local legislators, and the legislators would assure them that, of course, they agreed with the overall goals of the group, but that they couldn't commit to this or that piece of legislation without very specific answers or pieces of information. And our members would dutifully record all these questions and leave with no commitment for action.

So we did what most well-meaning advocates would do. We wrote more detailed fact sheets. We went out to the churches to do additional presentations. We held webinar briefings on all our issues, open to anyone interested. We tried to collect more academic studies. And a few people did attend these, but, overall, this didn't seem to solve the problem. There was always another unanswered question.

After going through this cycle for several large-scale actions with the same disappointing results, we finally changed course. We recognized that we can never know everything and answer every question. And people of faith shouldn't be expected to be professional-level policy analysts. What we needed to do instead was to get comfortable with moving in uncertainty. We do the best research we can, but there will always be unknowns. If we let that fact deter us, we will never take action. So the continual push for more information is really a way to delay action, perhaps indefinitely.

Instead of constantly providing more and more information, refuting every contrary study, the leaders in the Unitarian

Universalist churches focused on their relationships and their justice values. And they consciously talked about the need to "move in uncertainty." In fact, some congregations named this as a value they would hold.

These more affluent, generally white congregations, respected and valued the intelligence of people and communities most directly affected by injustice. If people with records were calling for something to improve their lives, the Unitarian Universalist churches decided that it was their job, as people committed to justice and solidarity, to stand with them. Instead of continually responding to information requests by hunting down new studies, they began bringing the questioner back to their key values and the relationship they had built.

So instead of saying, "That's a really good question. I'll look into that and get back to you and then maybe you'll consider coming to our public meeting?," we can say, "That's a fair question, but it's more important that we as a church stand up for justice and honor the voices of the people closest to the problem. Those people are calling for this change to happen. Are you willing to join our church in standing with them?"

That shift didn't change everything. There were still members who simply refused to act because they didn't know enough. But it did start moving more people into action, and it took away the need for the congregational leaders and organizing staff to continually go out digging into more and more research.

Intellectual curiosity and thoroughness of research are good things. But when they begin to be an obstacle to action, they are often masking a hesitancy to take risks or move outside our comfort zones. Many people have done research and been thoughtful about their needs. While we can never be 100 percent sure they, and we, are right, we cannot let these doubts stop us from acting.

Are you ready to respond, like James and John, to the call for justice? Are you ready to move in uncertainty?

Known by Our Fruits

When talking about trees being known by their fruits in the scripture that begins this chapter, I think Jesus is telling us that, as we become powerful agents of the kingdom, we must accept our duty to win. We need to be willing to engage with people outside of our comfort zone, live in the real world, make real concrete change, and move in uncertainty.

It can be comfortable to not be powerful. Then all we are required to do is to complain, say the right things, and share the right graphics on Facebook. But we are called to more. Jesus is telling us that God is calling us not just to think or say the right things but to produce good fruit—to really create change and move the world toward God's kingdom. Activist Assata Shakur said, "It is our duty to fight for our freedom. It is our duty to win." The poet and activist Marianne Deborah Williamson famously wrote (in a quote often attributed to Nelson Mandela), "Our deepest fear is not that we are inadequate. Our deepest fear is that we are powerful beyond measure. It is our light, not our darkness, that most frightens us. We ask ourselves, Who am I to be brilliant, gorgeous, talented, and fabulous? Actually, who are you not to be? You are a child of God. You're playing small does not serve the world."

Are you ready to accept this responsibility of being powerful and bearing good fruit?

CHAPTER 12

Wise as Serpents

Creating a Strategy to Win Change

Be wise as serpents and as innocent as doves.
—Matthew 10:16

When Jesus sends his disciples out by twos, preparing his followers to engage with the world, they must literally face an oppressive occupying force (the Romans) as well as a corrupt and complicit local leadership class (the chief priests and the scribes). So he gives them these instructions: "Behold, I am sending you like sheep in the midst of wolves; so be wise as serpents and as innocent as doves."

Most of us have no problem imagining ourselves as doves—beautiful birds of peace that convey God's love to all we meet. But seeing ourselves as serpents, even wise ones? That's harder. The serpent is the animal that tricks Adam and Eve into eating the forbidden fruit and being cast out of Eden. Since when has describing someone as a snake ever been a compliment?

That's probably why, whenever I have heard this scripture cited by Christians in the sphere of politics, social change, and the public world, it is most often with regard to ensuring that we remain innocent as doves, that our motives are pure, our hearts are untainted by anger, and that we are bringers of peace.

It's a beautiful message, of course, but too often we stop right there. We say that people of faith engaged in justice work must be *only* as innocent as doves, that any form of strategizing, counting votes, studying what will move a specific elected official or analyzing policy models and outcomes will taint us. We should simply stand up in the public square and share our powerful witness and call down God's justice from above.

And, in reality, this is what many churches and faith-based advocacy efforts do. My former pastor, and a champion for social justice, Father Larry Dowling, the pastor of St. Agatha Catholic Church in Chicago, experienced this himself.

It didn't take long for me to realize when I became a pastor in the North Lawndale neighborhood that shootings and killings were an all too real and regular occurrence in the community. The initial reaction is to march. Organize residents to stand up against the violence, the drugs, and the gangs in the community. It didn't take long before one gang member who chose to reach out to me explained that the marches only infuriated the gangs and other individuals who, in the face of being unable to get a regular job because of criminal records, were forced to sell drugs in order to support themselves and their families. What they needed, he 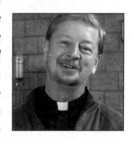 *told me, were legitimate living-wage jobs and education. Multiple forces were working against them: a society that continued to discriminate against them in jobs and housing, racism, and an unjust criminal justice system and local law "enforcement" that seemed to make every effort to re-incarcerate them.*

This led me pretty quickly to involve my congregation in faith-based community organizing with a particular focus on addressing these issues. Within the larger metro-Chicago/Cook County organization, we engaged the Reclaim Campaign: Repairing Jus-

tice, Restoring Lives, Rebuilding Communities. Through a comprehensive power analysis, we realized that the powerbrokers that we needed to engage, challenge, and transform were centered in Chicago City Hall with the mayor, in the Cook County board president and board of commissioners, in the office of the chief judge of Cook County, in the Cook County state's attorney, and in the local Cook County sheriff. A power analysis of each helped us to design specific strategies that would put public (political) pressure on each of the parties. Every approach was different, but always built from an understanding of policy, identifying leaders to engage with in initial meetings, some of which came easy, some of which required great pressure from a critical mass of organized leaders, then moving toward mutual agreements and implementation, and, in some cases, having leaders monitor promised changes.

One collectively decided approach as an organization was to work toward significantly decreasing the number of individuals sitting in jail by increasing the percentage of I-bonds (giving monitored release) from 20 percent to 70 percent, decreasing the amount of time someone had to sit in jail before a preliminary hearing from thirty days to five days, working to close two buildings at the Cook County jail and to use the savings to enhance our work in expanding restorative-justice (RJ) principles and practices in our communities through local schools, in the police department, and in our court system. This also called for us to challenge the other power players: to provide more funds for increasing education and the practice of RJ (Cook County funds); to reform court procedures and state's attorney practices; to challenge the mayor to undertake significant police reforms.

Through our work on the Reclaim Campaign, St. Agatha has established itself as a restorative justice hub, providing support and resources for resolution of conflict in local schools, in gang and individual conflict situations, and in families and the work-

place; increasing communication and conflict-resolution skills between parents and children; creating a network of support between parents and families; and building toward an organized group of families to stand together in demanding support for the education, health care, housing, and employment that they and their children deserve.

What Father Dowling learned is that Jesus instructs us to be both the serpent and the dove. We need both to hold God's peace and love in our hearts, refusing to become cynical or apathetic, and, at the same time, to bring all of our intelligence, craftiness, and knowledge to our work. Rather than simply marching down Main Street, or showing up at the first politicians' town hall we can find, we create a power analysis of the issue we are confronting. To be wise as serpents, we honestly assess our own organization and all the stakeholders in the arena. We must build a strategy, a concrete plan of a campaign to create the change we want to see in the world. As the old saying goes, "A failure to plan is a plan to fail!"

There are dozens of different tools for strategy and power analysis out there, and many of them have real advantages to them, so there is no one perfect formula; but here is a classic, five-step tool that can take you and your church from wanting to take action to having a real strategy, just like St. Agatha and the churches they partnered with.

1. What Do We Want?

This is a deceptively complicated question. It requires us to be specific and clear. We have to go deeper than "to end poverty" or "reduce homelessness," because we need to understand the real change we are trying to make and ensure that we have a chance to actually achieve it. In short, we are cutting a concrete *issue* out of a broad, amorphous *problem*.

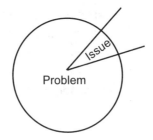

Problems are large, societal situations with no clear solution. Poverty, racism, violence, and war are all problems. And when we try to organize against problems, we rarely get very far. We have to get to specific solutions that cut manageable slices out of problems and move us closer to the kingdom. We call this slice or demand the issue. An ancient African proverb states: how do you eat an elephant? One bite at a time! Cutting clear issues out of overarching and amorphous problems follows this same wisdom.

To help figure out whether or not we really know what we want, there are three key questions to ask:

- Is it specific? If we were sitting at a table with the decision maker, and they said, "Okay, I'm ready to make change! What do you want me to do?" could we give them a clear, unambiguous answer that could be written down as law or policy? If we don't specifically know what change we want to make, we are liable to get nothing, or something worthless.
- Is it meaningful? By this we mean, does it create real change in the lives of real people? And, as discussed in our chapter on listening, to know if something is meaningful to people, we have to talk to them. Most people do not have time for symbolic victories. Especially when working with marginalized people, churches and people of faith need to be serious about actually making their lives better.

- Is it potentially winnable? With our organization, do we have enough power to potentially make this change happen? A single church alone is unlikely to be able to end mass incarceration or change a city ordinance, so if we decide that is our goal, we are either setting our people up for failure or we need to build partnerships with other churches and organizations!

2. Who Can "Give" It to Us?

The word "give" is in quotes, because, as Frederick Douglass said, "Power concedes nothing without a demand." But, nonetheless, when we have figured out the specific change we want to see, we need to figure out who the real-life person in authority is who has the power to make this decision.

Why is that so important? Well, it is embarrassing to march into your city council person's office because you are upset about the funding of your schools only to discover that those decisions are made at the state level! Put simply, if we don't understand where the decisions are made and by whom, we stand a poor chance of actually having an impact.

Organizers often refer to the decision maker (or decision makers) as the target, the person at whom our advocacy is aimed. There are people of faith who struggle with this term, feeling that it calls to mind a gun or violent image. It never did that for me. Maybe because when I grew up running track, "target" always was the goal I was trying to achieve and did not evoke a violent image for me. I suppose that if the word bothers you deeply, you can find another word, but spending your time obsessing about the use of a term and even insisting that other people change their language to accommodate your comfort probably falls into the purity-code area from the previous chapter.

In any event, we need to understand whom we are trying to influence and move.

3. Who Else Cares about This?

Issues do not exist in isolation. Organized people and organized money shape every issue and decision that gets made, and, if we hope to be effective, we need to understand everyone on the playing field. We call these people stakeholders—any person or organization who has a vested interest in the issue we care about. We need to understand what their interest is (do they share our concern? Oppose it? Or are they somewhere in between?), and how much influence the group has. Stakeholders that share our view on the issue are called allies. Stakeholders that hold a contrary position are called opponents or enemies. If we want to really make change, we cannot build a strategy that does not take into account what other forces are at play, so a good analysis of stakeholders is crucial.

Again, many people of faith have struggled with the term enemies, but, I, for one, strongly advocate for it. Why? Because, as Pastor Fields shared in the chapter on conflict, we will have enemies, and any strategy that does not take into account the people pushing against us is going to be missing many key elements. Perhaps even more importantly, whenever we hear the word "enemy," as followers of Christ we have to think of Jesus's teaching on loving one's enemies. Using the word forces me, as a Christian, to not dehumanize the opposition.

4. Understand the Decision Maker

Okay, I'm going to cheat. This is actually three questions, but they are all related. Once we know who our target is, we need to understand what moves that person or set of people. So really, after doing a power analysis of the issue that we are concerned with, we need to do a power analysis of the target. A simple way to do this is to answer three questions:

- What does our target want?
- What does our target fear?
- With whom is our target in relationship?

Answering these three questions will help us form the outlines of a campaign that has a real chance to win. Any campaign that doesn't give a target something they want, threaten them with something they fear, or impact one or several of their key relationships has very little chance of winning.

Almost a decade ago, a coalition that included a number of faith leaders and groups in Chicago was trying to move Mayor Daley to protect public housing developments and create new affordable housing. The coalition could mobilize several hundred people and was pushing the mayor with a message that housing was a human right. These were passionate, committed, and faithful people, but, I'm sorry to say, they didn't have a lot of success in their campaign. Why? Because what they were doing didn't impact what the mayor cared about. I had seen very little evidence that a key concern of Mayor Daley and the Chicago political machine was human rights, and mobilizing hundreds, or even a few thousand, people across a city of millions didn't threaten the mayor's chances of re-election. Despite our best intentions, the coalition did not succeed in protecting the housing of thousands of low-income Chicagoans, and many lost their housing, became homeless, or simply disappeared. All because we didn't have a good power analysis of our target.

On the other hand, Father Dowling and the Reclaim Campaign constructed a careful power analysis of each of their targeted decision makers and used strategies and messages specifically tailored to move each target. As a result, thousands of fewer people are now sitting in Cook County jail, and communities across the city have resources to build their own peace-making initiatives.

5. What Tactics Can We Honestly Execute That Will Move Our Target?

Finally, with a full understanding of what we are hoping to achieve, who can give it to us, what they want, and who else is on the playing field, we can plan tactics—specific activities to move our target to take action and address the issue that we are working on.

Most organizers and activists love tactics; we are excited about moving into action, and we should be. Actions are what we picture when we think about social justice. Picket lines, marches, public mass meetings, and lobby days at the state capitol! Let's do it!

There are whole books just on planning actions, but for now, here are three crucial things we need to remember. First, tactics must come out of a power analysis and strategy. Second, they have to be within our actual capability to pull off. And third, actions must be within the general experience of our people and as outside of the general experience of our target as possible.

The first of these rules is fairly obvious. Even really large and exciting tactics will fail if they don't impact what our targets care about, as in the case of Mayor Daley presented earlier. This is one of the reasons we ask this question about tactics last. We cannot know if a tactic is a good or bad idea until we understand the person or people we are trying to move with it. For instance, as a faith-based community, many of my organization's actions used to include prayer processions, often with a cross. This tactic made sense in a number of places when we had a Roman Catholic mayor of Chicago and governor of Illinois, both of whom were used to these sort of processions at weekly Mass. However, when Rahm Emanuel, who is Jewish, was elected mayor, we realized this tactic had to change. Marching on a Jewish person behind a cross wouldn't have the same impact, and, in fact, given the history of persecution of the Jewish people by Christian churches, could be highly offensive. We needed to find different religious imagery to speak to a new target.

In the same way, even the most brilliant idea for an action will fail miserably if we can't pull it off. I can't tell you how many tables I have sat at where people are so upset about something that they plan a march or rally, only to realize that they can only get a few dozen people to go along with them. It's almost always better to start with smaller tactics that you are sure you can handle and then build toward larger ones (using the principle of escalation from the previous chapter). Don't start by calling for a boycott on a store if we know that we can't communicate with most of their patrons and don't have enough picket teams to be out front during all the key shopping times. Instead, start with having a small delegation ask for a meeting with the manager. Then move to a few informational pickets outside the store. Then start a phone tree for call-in days. Then call for a one-day boycott, when you are sure that you can get a large number of people outside. Each of these tactics can build on the previous one, and, by succeeding in smaller ones, you can build power toward bigger ones.

The third rule, that an action should be within the general experience of our members and as far as possible outside the experience of our target, is a little less obvious. I once was part of a coalition planning a big public meeting with the president of the school board. We were demanding that the student code of conduct be changed to remove long suspensions and insert restorative justice disciplinary practices in response to findings that African American males were being suspended and expelled at disproportionate rates. It was a diverse coalition and included a number of churches that I was organizing as well as youth groups, teachers, and community activists, some of whom were used to more confrontational tactics. As we discussed what to do if the president said no to the demands of the coalition, most of the groups decided that they wanted to boo her and end the meeting. It became clear that some of my churches didn't feel comfortable with that, but we pushed ahead. I guess, we were hoping it wouldn't come up.

Boy, were we wrong! Not only did the president not say yes, she flat out lied and said that she has never heard of these demands and asked why we were making the ask of her. Groups of people started booing, and she walked out on the hundreds of people in the room. I could see the faces of some of the church members who were attending. They were *not* happy! They were mad at us for inviting them to what they saw as an unfair and uncivil action. Booing someone was not within their experience. And being booed by (and then walking out on) a rowdy crowd was totally normal for the school board president. Ouch! What a lesson.

But at least we learned something. A year later, our organization was planning an even bigger public meeting with the governor and members of the state assembly. We were asking the governor to unfreeze a fund holding over $20 million for housing for low-income people, and we were calling on the general assembly to pass legislation to seal nonviolent criminal records so people could get jobs. This meeting would be in a church and in the sanctuary itself, so I knew that people would be even less comfortable with yelling and booing. At the same time, we knew we needed to make the action powerful and to show the officials that we meant business so they would take the demands for school funding, affordable housing, and criminal justice reform seriously. We also knew that the governor was running for re-election and would need the votes of black churches in the coming months.

Remembering the disaster months before, we came up with two new ideas. We would not chant and yell. Instead we would use the powerful tradition of singing to make a loud and powerful noise. It was easy to get one thousand church folks on their feet and clapping to praise songs they knew, and just as easy to add verses about the actual issues we were addressing. Those officials would walk into a room with the rafters shaking!

Even more important, we needed a plan for elected officials who refused to sign onto the platform that our churches had developed, and we knew that booing wouldn't work. Then it hit us! We might not like booing, but we *loved* praying. If the key decision maker said no or refused to give a clear answer to our questions, we could engage in prayer. So we set a plan! If one of the legislators refused to commit to our platform, we would have the entire congregation stand, raise their hands and lead a call-and-response prayer for God to change that person's heart! And for the governor, we planned something even more special! If he didn't say yes, we would ask the whole congregation to stand and raise their hands and silently pray for God to change the governor's heart. And we wouldn't stop! We would hold the space with the power of prayer until the governor agreed to release the millions of dollars for affordable housing that he was currently withholding. This sort of thing was totally normal for our members. Praying, singing, and laying hands in church was something they did every Sunday. The Bible tells us to pray without ceasing, and there are any numbers of examples of how prayer changes things. Our people loved the idea!

But can you imagine? What would the governor do? Try to interrupt one thousand praying people? Storm out on prayer? Just keep standing there awkwardly? He had never faced this particular dilemma before! It was completely outside of his experience.

I'm almost sorry to say that we didn't get to exercise this particular tactic. The governor agreed to release the funds. But we did get to do the call-and-response prayer over a legislator; and, in fact, one of his fellow legislators joined us and laid hands on his colleague in prayer! It's still one of my favorite organizing memories. The huge praise and worship meeting with a prayer response became a staple of our actions. We had found a way to use who we were and what our people knew to our advantage. And all because we had done careful planning and thought about tactics that made sense for our people and would properly impact our targets!

So there you have it, five steps to build a strategy to win real change. These kinds of carefully crafted campaigns and tactics give us the wisdom of serpents, the tools to wiggle through any obstacle to make sure that we achieve the justice God has called us to, without ever losing touch of our dovish innocence, of profound faith, hope, and love.

When your congregation engages a campaign, do you know who the key decision makers are? Do you have a strategy that will actually affect them, or do you count on your purity of heart and motive alone? Are you ready to take Jesus's full directive to heart and do the hard, snake-like work of strategy development?

Walk Forth!

As I write this, children fleeing violence are locked up in intern-
ment camps on the United States–Mexico border. Our country
is teetering on the verge of another war in the Middle East that
will cost thousands of civilian lives. The U.S. Congress passed a
massive tax bill, focusing on about a trillion dollars in tax cuts
for corporations and the tiniest sliver of the wealthiest Ameri-
cans, while setting in motion plans to eviscerate programs that
millions of low-income and working families rely on to keep
their families afloat and even to survive. The president has risen
to power by attacking immigrants, women, and people of color;
nearly all the people that Jesus and the prophets stood for. There
has never been a more important time for the church to be a
truly powerful force for God's justice.

But I see hope. I see hope because across the country, people who have never taken action before are beginning to stand
up. I see hope because new and exciting alliances are forming
locally and across the country. In Illinois, I was privileged to
help lead a newly energized push to amend our state's constitution to create a progressive income tax, which will go before
voters in 2020. Teacher strikes across the country have created
better schools for children and justice for hard-working educa-
tors. I see hope because whenever I'm called to speak, preach, or
train at a church, I hear new people saying that they want to do

something. And I see hope because I've been asked to write this book, and because you are reading it.

It's my prayer for you that you now have the tools to help transform your passion and desire into concrete action to build powerful churches and create real change in your community and our country. God has called you, and you already have everything you need to get started.

Like Dale Griffin, you can summon up your courage and schedule five one-on-ones with people in your congregation who might share your passion. Use these relationships to build a team around you, as Christina Rice has done. Share this book with them or identify training you need to develop your leadership skills like Teleza Rodgers. Move people into action and leadership through powerful agitation, like Rachel Lyons learned. Engage your whole church and community through a broad listening campaign like Rev. Robert Biekman, and prioritize the voices of people directly affected, like Eddie Bocanegra.

As you come together, make the shift from providing charity to becoming public advocates for justice, like Jiquanda Nelson. Be willing to confront injustice with prophetic resistance, the way Rev. Cy Fields does. Own the fact that you and your church want to be powerful, the way Rev. Alan Taylor does. Build a wise strategy to address the issues that matter to you, the way Father Dowling does. And create alliances with other groups and live in the real world in order to make change, the way Katelyn Johnson does.

Each of these people shared their story not because they are unique but because they are like you, pastors and lay leaders who want to move differently in the world. They have utilized the tools of organizing to transform their lives, their churches, and their communities. You picked this book up because you are one of the millions of people who want to make a difference and didn't know how. Or maybe you didn't believe that you could. But people and churches just like you have, and are, responding to God's call right now. You, too, can sit down, face to face with someone and start building power.

Even more importantly, you aren't doing this work in isolation. Across the country, there are faith-based organizing groups. Many are affiliated with some of the national networks, including the PICO Network, Gamaliel Foundation, and Industrial Areas Foundation. And there are even more issue-based groups and nonfaith-based groups that would love to partner with your church—once you have become a powerful force that can develop leaders, turn large numbers of people out, and hold elected officials accountable.

None of these groups are perfect. Neither is this book. And your efforts won't be either. But doing nothing because you can't be perfect is exactly what the devil and the forces of injustice would like you to do. Remember the Romero prayer, and go and start building power. Build one relationship at a time. Shift your congregation's focus to include concrete action for justice. Win one small victory and move on to the next.

At a retreat on the Sermon on the Mount, I once was told that, while we usually translate the Beatitudes as "blessed are," perhaps an even better translation would be "walk forth." Jesus isn't giving a passive affirmation; he is offering a benediction, a call to action, a blessing of the path people are called to walk.

So walk forth, all of you whose hearts are crying out for justice. Walk forth to move from charity to justice. Walk forth as a leader of a powerful congregation.

The lines from Jesus's first public sermon are for all of us: The spirit of the Lord is upon all of us, for God has anointed us to bring good news to the poor, to proclaim freedom to captives and recovery of sight to the blind. To set the oppressed free and to proclaim God's justice and jubilee!

We can transform our churches, and our churches can change the world.

Sample One-on-One Report-Back Form

One-on-one conducted by:	
Date:	
Church member I spoke with:	
Phone/email:	
What did I learn about this person's story?	
How do they understand the role of their faith, justice, and the values of our congregation?	
What is their self-interest? What specific issues do they care about?	
What vision did I cast? What action did I propose?	
What strengths and leadership potential do I see in this person?	
Reflection—What did I learn about myself in this one-on-one?	

Sample House Meeting Agenda with Justice Bible Study

Opening Prayer, Introductions, and Background Information (5 minutes)

- **Who are we and why are we here?** Go around the circle and introduce ourselves.
- **Why is our church holding house meetings?** Local congregations set the agenda by identifying the key issues that are affecting our communities. We are holding house meetings to get to know the people in our congregations and neighborhoods, identify new leaders, and learn about important issues that we can come together around and fight to change. We are here to identify concrete things we can do to improve our church, neighborhood, city, and state.

Our Faith and Social Action (15 minutes)

In groups of about five, answer the following questions using our Bibles as a resource:

1. Find two places in the Old Testament law books where the people of God are commanded to care for the poor and vulnerable.
2. Find two places where the prophets tell the leaders of Israel that God cares about how they treat the poor, widow, orphan, stranger, and oppressed.
3. Identify three of Jesus's parables that are about how we should treat others.

4. Name two places in scripture where Jesus breaks the rules or challenges current practices because they are not fair to the poor and the outcast.
5. Find the place in the letter of James where he discusses the difference between faith and works. What is the relationship between the two?

What can we conclude by answering these questions? What does our faith call us to?

Stories and Sharing (15 minutes)

Pair off, introduce yourselves, and ask:

- What do you love about your neighborhood or church?
- What challenges have you seen or experienced recently?
- What one or two specific things would you most want to change?
- Why are those things important to you?

Sharing and Key Problems (20–30 minutes)

Come back together and report on your conversations.

- What key problems did people identify?
- Where can we find common ground?
- Do other people have similar stories or experiences?

Commitments and Action Plan (15 minutes)

- Who would participate or help to coordinate a meeting like this around each of the priority issues we identified?
- Is there any research we need to do in advance of that meeting? Who can do it?
- Who will attend our church's closing meeting to plan action around the issues we have identified?

Review of Commitments, Next Steps, and Closing Prayer

Sample Organizing Campaign Guide and a Sample Plan

Tools of Organizing Drives

Use the tools of organizing drives to strengthen your church, build relationships among members, identify new leaders, learn about the needs of your community, and assess the ministry needs of your church. Building a congregational organizing plan can include a mix of these organizing tools.

Building a Congregational Organizing Plan

- **Set Your Goals.** What do you want for your church? Is it to engage more of the existing membership? Learn about your community? Move people into action? Take some time to think about what makes sense for your congregation at this point in time. Then select the tools that make the most sense for these goals.
- **Identify Who, What, and When.** It is vital to know what leaders are going to carry out the plan, what organizing tools you are going to employ, and a start and end date. Most plans should be eight to twelve weeks long and have at least one check-in point for your entire team. It may be helpful to scale back some other congregational activities to give adequate attention to your plan and to explore partnering with other, nearby congregations if your plans overlap.
- **What Training Do You Need?** What are the skills the leaders in your congregation need to develop to make your plan

successful? Make sure you set aside time to receive training in these skills.

- **Engage the Entire Church.** It's important to let your entire congregation know what is happening. Announcements should be made in advance of any organizing drive. Leaders who are going to be carrying out the plan should be publicly identified and commissioned during worship. And the entire church should be invited to learn about the process and to attend your final meetings.

- **Hold a Closing Meeting.** At the end of your plan, hold a closing meeting open to all members of your congregation. Set concrete next steps to move forward based on what you have learned. What are the new projects or issues you will begin (or the long-standing ones that you will end)? What are you going to ask newly identified or energized leaders to do?

Organizing Tools You Can Use

One-on-Ones/Relational Meetings

One-on-ones are at the core of congregational organizing. These intentional thirty- to forty-minute meetings are a chance to build relationships with members of the congregation, identify new potential leaders, or learn where members might be willing to exert leadership. One-on-ones can be excellent tools to learn about new members of your congregation as well as long-standing members. They are a terrific chance to move people to step into leadership roles.

House Meetings

House meetings are gatherings of five to twenty-five people that last between an hour and an hour and a half. Despite their name, they can be held in homes, your church, or even a local park or coffee shop. In these meetings, we draw out people's stories and learn about what is happening in our congregations and communities. House meetings can be used as stand-alone organizing tools, or you can hold house meetings around specific topics that have been identified through an earlier round of house meetings, one-on-ones, or canvassing.

Neighborhood Canvassing

Neighborhood door-to-door canvassing is a tool that many churches use to get to know the people and the needs of the community immediately surrounding the church. Listening to our neighborhood can be an excellent way to grow our churches and expand our relationships. After a round of canvassing, it usually makes sense to have a plan of one-on-ones or house meetings to follow up with the new people and on issues you have identified through your canvassing.

Organizing Drive Planning Sheet

Goals _____

_____

_____

_____

_____

_____

Leaders _____

_____

_____

Tools _____

_____

Timeline _____

Training Needed _____

_____

_____

Plan to Engage Broader Church _____

_____

_____

Closing Meeting Date _____

Sample Congregational Organizing Plan

Note: This is a fairly advanced plan that goes beyond the initial outreach timeline into issues and action. It also includes a list of roles and their descriptions.

Goal: The goal of this project is to engage a broader set of community members, develop their leadership skills, and build power for our church to take action on local, city, and state issues.

Stage 1—Initial Outreach—Six Weeks

Goal: Engage disengaged church members and people who had previously been involved in church programming as well as local residents.

Steps: 1. Introduce plan to parenting class graduation and church.
2. One-on-one training
3. Street outreach training
4. One-on-ones during Mass
5. Have a ten-person team of people do five one-on-ones each (one per week) for a total of fifty conversations with disengaged members/participants. The goal of these conversations is to:
   a. rebuild a relationship with the members
   b. identify the issues that they are most concerned with, the needs they have, and the gifts they can contribute to our work, and
   c. invite them to take some action.
6. Hold three neighborhood canvasses, every other Saturday.

Stage 2—Issue Engagement—Four to Six Weeks

Goal: Identify key issues of concern for our community and set an action plan.

Steps: 1. Hold issue training sessions for key leaders covering the criteria for identifying an issue, and the steps to leading a caucus circle.
2. Hold an issue caucus meeting. We will bring all the people who expressed interest through our one-on-ones and canvasses together, lay out the vision of our work, and have people caucus around key issues of concern to clarify the issue and brainstorm initial steps.
3. Hold one to two additional canvasses around the issues we identified.
4. Each issue caucus holds one follow up meeting.

Stage 3—Begin Campaigns and Outreach Program—One to Two Months

Goal: Launch campaigns to win victories for our neighborhood and create an ongoing outreach program.

Steps: 1. Hold a campaign training session, including basic power analysis and action steps.
2. Hold a "train the trainers" for street outreach captains.
3. Launch street outreach team with a monthly canvass where we
   a. let people know about the current work we are doing,
   b. ask them about current issues/concerns,
   c. invite them to take some immediate action, and
   d. follow up with a call to invite them to a relevant action/activity.
4. Issue teams solidify campaigns and plan initial action steps/meetings.

Stage 4—Actions and Development—Two to Three Months

Goal: Move our campaigns into action and set a strategy for developing local leadership

Steps: 1. Plan and execute an initial action for our campaigns (we may have joined forces with possible partner organizations at this point).
2. Training on second one-on-ones
3. Launch relational interview team—ten members who do two to three one-on-ones per month with people who have been identified as potential leaders to engage them and connect them to action.
4. Hold evaluation and planning retreat at the end of the year.

Key Roles/ Job Descriptions

Street Outreach Team

Responsibilities: Hold one canvass per month (initially three in six weeks) to meet community members, identify their concerns, and connect them to the work of the church and project.
Do follow-up calls a few days after each canvass to invite people to participate in an action.

Training Needed: Canvass training (two to three hours total)

Street Outreach Team Captain

Responsibilities: Plan route and canvass
Train/review canvassing techniques with members
Hold one-on-ones with potential new members

Training Needed: Street outreach team "train the trainers"

Relational Interview Team

Responsibilities: Hold one one-on-one meeting (thirty to forty minutes) per week with church/community members to build relationship, identify needs and strengths, and to engage them in local action and a leadership development plan.

Training Needed: One-on-ones training; Leadership development one-on-ones training

Callers

Responsibilities: Call people from canvasses and other activities to update them on project and invite them to actions and events.

Child Care/Food Team

Responsibilities: Prepare food and provide child care during project activities to allow families to participate.

Issue Caucus Leaders

Responsibilities: Lead issue caucuses, house meetings, and circles around areas of concern.
Focus the group and move to clear action steps.
Provide detailed notes for follow up.

Training Needed: Issue training

Campaign Leaders

Responsibilities: Lead campaign activities and strategy.

Training Needed: Must have been members of another teamcampaign training

Powerful Congregation Checklist

Does my congregation . . .

- Have a team of leaders organizing the church?

- Do regular one-on-ones and/or house meetings?

- Regularly communicate justice and organizing work to the entire church?

- Have a process to identify and focus on key issues?

- Utilize a leadership ladder?

- Have a clear understanding and process for how someone gets the authority to lead?

- Hold people mutually accountable for their commitments?

- Analyze power and put our efforts into winnable actions or campaigns?

A Sample Agenda
from an Accountability Session

Goal: To win commitments from our legislators to support the initiatives in the Platform for Renewal

10:00   **Opening Prayer and Welcome**

10:05   **Opening Music—"He Has Done Marvelous"**

10:10   **Occasion/Purpose of the Day**

10:15   **Responsive Reading**

10:20   **Music and Collection—"Victory Is Mine"**

10:30   **Welcome of Elected Officials**

10:40   **Guidelines for the Agenda/Recognition of Churches**

10:50   **Presentation of the Issues**
- Expanding of sealing of felony records
- Stopping illegal gun trafficking—youth testimony
- Fair tax for education funding

11:05   **Prayer over the Platform**
- Prayer in Spanish
- Prayer in English

11:15 **Legislative Endorsement of the Platform for Renewal**
- Each legislator will be asked, "Will you commit to supporting this platform, yes or no?"
- Each legislator will be asked to come forward and sign a large copy of the platform

11:30 **Comments from Legislators**

11:45 **Call to Action/Benediction**

Index